*...ughn*

English ASAP™

Connecting English to the Workplace

SCANS Consultant

Shirley Brod
Spring Institute for International Studies
Boulder, Colorado

Program Consultants

Judith Dean-Griffin
ESL Teacher
Windham Independent School District
Texas Department of Criminal Justice
Huntsville, Texas

Marilyn K. Spence
Workforce Education Coordinator
Orange Technical Education Centers
Mid-Florida Tech
Orlando, Florida

Brigitte Marshall
English Language Training
for Employment Participation
Albany, California

Dennis Terdy
Director, Community Education
Township High School District 214
Arlington Heights, Illinois

Christine Kay Williams
ESL Specialist
Towson University
Baltimore, Maryland

STECK-VAUGHN
ELEMENTARY · SECONDARY · ADULT · LIBRARY

A Harcourt Company

www.steck-vaughn.com

Acknowledgments

Executive Editor: Ellen Northcutt

Supervising Editor: Tim Collins

Assistant Art Director: Richard Balsam

Interior Design: Richard Balsam, Jill Klinger, Paul Durick

Electronic Production: Jill Klinger, Stephanie Stewart, Alan Klemp

Assets Manager: Margie Foster

Editorial Development: Course Crafters, Inc., Newburyport, Massachusetts

Photo Credits

Alhadeff–p.6, 15, 27, 34-35, 46-47, 51, 58-59, 63c, 75c, 75d, 94-95, 106-107, 111b, 114a, 118-119; Don Couch Photography–p.39a, 39c, 39d, 111c, 111d; Jack Demuth–3b, 3c, 13, 39b, 92a, 92b, 92c, 99b; Patrick Dunn–p.87a, 87b, 111a, 114b; Christine Galida–p.61, 63a, 63d, 75a, 87c, 107b; David Omer–p.22-23, 82-83; Sharon Seligman–p.75b, 87d; Park Street–p.3a, 3d, 10-11, 28, 53, 70-71, 99a, 99c, 99d, 101.

Additional photography: p. 63b ©Superstock.

Illustration Credits

Cover: Tim Dove, D Childress

Cindy Aarvig–p.30, 37, 64, 88, 97a; Richard Balsam–p.10-12, 14, 17-20, 22a, 23-25, 35, 55, 57-59, 62, 138; Barbara Beck–p.70-72, 74, 76, 85; Antonio Castro (Represented by Cornell & McCarthy, LLC)–p.113; Chris Celusniak–p.29, 95; Rhonda Childress–p.4, 9; David Griffin–p.16 , 22b-d, 26, 33, 52, 68, 93, 140, 142, 143; Dennis Harms–p.31, 34, 38; Chuck Joseph–p.77-79, 81-83, 85d, 86, 91, 94, 96, 106, 107a, 108, 109, 118-121; Linda Kelen–p.5, 144; Michael Krone–p.40, 49, 65, 97b-d, 98, 112; John Scott–p.90, 105; Charles Shaw–p. 136; Danielle Szabo–p.3, 15, 27, 36, 39, 41, 48, 49e, 50, 51, 56, 60, 63, 75, 87, 99, 111; Milburn Taylor–p.54, 66, 73, 89.

ISBN 0-8172-7951-2

Copyright © 1999 Steck-Vaughn Company

English ASAP is a trademark of Steck-Vaughn Company.

2 3 4 5 6 7 8 9 10 WC 02 01 00

Contents

About SCANS, the Workforce, and *English ASAP: Connecting English to the Workplace*

SCANS and the Workforce

The Secretary's Commission on Achieving Necessary Skills (SCANS) was established by the U.S. Department of Labor in 1990. Its mission was to study the demands of workplace environments and determine whether people entering the workforce are capable of meeting those demands. The commission identified skills for employment, suggested ways for assessing proficiency, and devised strategies to implement the identified skills. The commission's first report, entitled *What Work Requires of Schools—SCANS Report for America 2000,* was published in June 1991. The report is designed for use by educators (curriculum developers, job counselors, training directors, and teachers) to prepare the modern workforce for the workplace with viable, up-to-date skills.

The report identified two types of skills: Competencies and Foundations. There are five SCANS Competencies: (1) Resources, (2) Interpersonal, (3) Information, (4) Systems, and (5) Technology. There are three parts contained in SCANS Foundations: (1) Basic Skills (including reading, writing, arithmetic, mathematics, listening, and speaking); (2) Thinking Skills (including creative thinking, decision making, problem solving, seeing things in the mind's eye, knowing how to learn, and reasoning); and (3) Personal Qualities (including responsibility, self-esteem, sociability, self-management, and integrity/honesty).

Steck-Vaughn's *English ASAP: Connecting English to the Workplace*

English ASAP is a complete SCANS-based, four-skills program for teaching ESL and SCANS skills to adults and young adults. *English ASAP* follows a work skills-based syllabus that is compatible with the CASAS and MELT competencies.

English ASAP is designed for learners enrolled in public or private schools, in corporate training environments, in learning centers, or in institutes, and for individuals working with tutors. *English ASAP* has these components:

Student Books

The Student Books are designed to allow from 125 to 235 hours of instruction. Each Student Book contains 10 units of SCANS-based instruction. A Listening Transcript of material appearing on the Audiocassettes and a Vocabulary list, organized by unit, of core workforce-based words and phrases appear at the back of each Student Book. Because unit topics carry over from level to level, *English ASAP* is ideal for multi-level classes.

The *On Your Job* symbol appears on the Student Book page each time learners apply a work skill to their own jobs or career interests.

An abundance of tips throughout each unit provides information and strategies that learners can use to be more effective workers and language learners.

Teacher's Editions

Teacher's Editions provide reduced Student Book pages with answers inserted and wraparound teacher notes that give detailed suggestions on how to present each page of the Student Book in class. Teacher's Editions 1 and 2 also provide blackline masters to reinforce the grammar in each unit. The Literacy Level Teacher's Edition contains blackline masters that provide practice with many basic literacy skills. The complete Listening Transcript, Vocabulary, and charts for tracking individual and class success appear at the back of each Teacher's Edition.

Workbooks

The Workbooks, starting at Level 1, provide reinforcement for each section of the Student Books.

Audiocassettes

The Audiocassettes contain all the dialogs and listening activities in the Student Books.

 This symbol appears on the Student Book page and corresponding Teacher's Edition page each time material for that page is recorded on the Audiocassettes. A Listening Transcript of all material recorded on the tapes but not appearing directly on the Student Book pages is at the back of each Student Book and Teacher's Edition.

Workforce Writing Dictionary

Steck-Vaughn's *Workforce Writing Dictionary*, is a 96-page custom dictionary that allows learners to create a personalized, alphabetical list of the key words and phrases they need to know for their jobs. Each letter of the alphabet is allocated two to four pages for learners to record the language they need. In addition, each letter is illustrated with several workforce-related words.

Placement Tests

The Placement Tests, Form A and Form B, can be used as entry and exit tests and to assist in placing learners in the appropriate level of *English ASAP*.

Placement

In addition to the Placement Tests, the following table indicates placement based on the CASAS and new MELT student performance level standards.

Placement

New MELT SPL	CASAS Achievement Score	English ASAP
0–1	179 or under	Literacy
2–3	180–200	Level 1
4–5	201–220	Level 2
6	221–235	Level 3
7	236 and above	Level 4

About Student Book 1

Organization of a Unit

Each twelve-page unit contains these nine sections: Unit Opener, Getting Started, Talk About It, Keep Talking, Listening, Grammar, Reading and Writing, Extension, and Performance Check.

Unit Opener

Each Unit Opener includes photos and several related, work-focused questions. The photos and questions activate learners' prior knowledge by getting them to think and talk about the unit topic. The **Performance Preview**, which gives an overview of all the skills in the unit, helps teachers set goals and purposes for the unit. Optionally, teachers may want to examine the Performance Preview with learners before they begin the unit.

Getting Started

An initial **Team Work** activity presents key work skills, concepts, and language introduced in the unit. It consists of active critical thinking and peer teaching to activate the use of the new language and to preview the content of the unit. A **Partner Work** or **Practice the**

To the Teacher

Dialog activity encourages learners to use the new language in communicative ways. A culminating class or group **Survey** encourages learners to relate the new language to themselves and their workplaces or career interests.

Talk About It

This page provides opportunities for spoken communication. **Practice the Dialog** provides a model for conversation. **Partner Work** presents a personalized **On Your Job** activity that allows learners to use the model in Practice the Dialog to talk about their own workplace experiences.

Useful Language | The **Useful Language** box contains related words, phrases, and expressions for learners to use as they complete Partner Work.

ASAP PROJECT The **ASAP Project** is a long-term project learners complete over the course of the unit. Learners create items such as files of human resources forms, lists of interview questions, and work schedules that they can use outside of the classroom.

Keep Talking

The Keep Talking page contains additional conversation models and speaking tasks. It also includes the **Personal Dictionary** feature. This feature allows learners to record the language relevant to the unit topic that they need to do their jobs. Because each learner's job is different, this personalized resource enables learners to focus on the language that is most useful to them. In addition, learners can use this feature in conjunction with Steck-Vaughn's *Workforce Writing Dictionary* to create a completely customized lexicon of key words and phrases they need to know.

Listening

The Listening page develops SCANS-based listening skills. Tasks include listening for greetings, names of places, directions, instructions, and times.

All the activities develop the skill of **focused listening.** Learners learn to recognize the information they need and to listen selectively for only that information. They do not have to understand every word; rather, they have to filter out everything except the relevant information. This essential skill is used by native speakers of all languages.

Many of the activities involve **multi-task listening.** In these activities, called **Listen Again** and **Listen Once More**, learners listen to the same selection several times and complete a different task each time. First they might listen for the main idea. They might listen again for specific information. They might listen a third time in order to draw conclusions or make inferences.

Culminating discussion questions allow learners to relate the information they have heard to their own needs and interests.

A complete Listening Transcript for all dialogs recorded on the Audiocassettes but not appearing directly on the Student Book pages is at the back of the Student Book and Teacher's Edition. All the selections are recorded on the Audiocassettes.

Grammar

Grammar, a two-page spread, presents key grammatical structures that complement the unit competencies. Language boxes show the new language in a clear, simple format that allows learners to make generalizations about the new language. Oral and written exercises provide contextualized reinforcement relevant to the workplace.

Reading and Writing

Reading selections, such as excerpts from instruction manuals, job evaluations, and timecards, focus on items learners encounter at work. Exercises and discussion questions develop reading skills and help learners relate the content of the selections to their workplaces or career interests.

The writing tasks, often related to the reading selection, help learners develop writing skills, such as completing job applications, writing to-do lists, and writing schedules.

Extension

The Extension page enriches the previous instruction. As in other sections, realia is used extensively. Oral and written exercises help learners master the additional skills, language, and concepts, and relate them to their workplaces and career interests.

Culture Notes **Culture Notes**, a feature that appears on each Extension page, sparks lively, engaging discussion. Topics include asking for directions, using machines, using employee handbooks, and exchanging greetings.

Performance Check

The two-page Performance Check allows teachers and learners to track learners' progress and to meet the learner verification needs of schools, companies, or programs. All work skills are tested in the same manner they are presented in the units; so, formats are familiar and non-threatening, and success is built in. The **Performance Review** at the end of each test alerts teachers and learners to the work skills that are being evaluated. The check-off boxes allow learners to track their success and gain a sense of accomplishment and satisfaction. Finally, a culminating discussion allows learners to relate their new skills to their development as effective workers.

Teaching Techniques

Make Your Classroom Mirror the Workplace

Help learners develop workplace skills by setting up your classroom to mirror a workplace. Use any of these suggestions.

◆ Establish policies on lateness and absence similar to those a business might have.

◆ Provide learners with a daily agenda of the activities they will complete that day, including partner work and small group assignments. Go over the agenda with learners at the beginning and end of class.

◆ With learner input, establish a list of goals for the class. Goals can include speaking, reading, and writing English every day; using effective teamwork skills; or learning ten new vocabulary words each day. Go over the goals with learners at regular intervals.

◆ Assign students regular jobs and responsibilities, such as arranging the chairs in a circle, setting up the overhead projector, or making copies for the class.

Presenting a Unit Opener

The unit opener sets the stage for the unit. Use the photos and questions to encourage learners to:

◆ Speculate about what the unit might cover.

◆ Activate prior knowledge.

◆ Relate what they see in the photos to their own work environments.

Peer Teaching

Because each adult learner brings rich life experience to the classroom, *English ASAP* is designed to help you use each learner's expertise as a resource for peer teaching.

Here are some practical strategies for peer teaching:

◆ Have learners work in pairs/small groups to clarify new language concepts for each other.

◆ If a learner possesses a particular work skill, appoint that learner as "class consultant" in that area and have learners direct queries to that individual.

To the Teacher

- Set up a reference area in a corner of your classroom. Include dictionaries, career books, and other books your learners will find useful.

Partner Work and Team Work

The abundance of Partner Work and Team Work activities in *English ASAP* serves the dual purposes of developing learners' communicative competence and providing learners with experience using key SCANS interpersonal skills, such as working in teams, teaching others, leading, negotiating, and working well with people from culturally diverse backgrounds. To take full advantage of these activities, follow these suggestions.

- Whenever students work in groups, appoint, or have students select, a leader.

- Use multiple groupings. Have learners work with different partners and teams, just as workers do in the workplace. For different activities, you might group learners according to language ability, skill, or learner interest.

- Make sure learners understand that everyone on the team is responsible for the team's work.

- At the end of each activity, have teams report the results to the class.

- Discuss with learners their teamwork skills and talk about ways teams can work together effectively. They can discuss how to clarify roles and responsibilities, resolve disagreements effectively, communicate openly, and make decisions together.

Purpose Statement

Each page after the unit opener begins with a brief purpose statement that summarizes the work skills presented on that page. When learners first begin working on a page, focus their attention on the purpose statement and help them read it. Ask them what the page will be about. Discuss with the class why the skill is important. Ask learners to talk about their prior knowledge of the skill. Finally, show learners how using the skill will help them become more effective on their jobs.

Survey

The **Survey** on each **Getting Started** page helps learners relate the new language and skills to their own lives. Before learners begin the activity, help them create questions they'll need to ask. Assist them in deciding how they'll record their answers. You may need to model taking notes, using tally marks, and other simple ways to record information. Assist learners in setting a time limit before they begin. Remember to allow learners to move about the room as they complete the activity.

Many Survey results can be summarized in a bar graph or pie chart.

- A bar graph uses bars to represent numbers. Bar graphs have two scales, a vertical scale and a horizontal scale. For example, to graph the number of learners who get paid by check versus those paid by direct deposit, the vertical scale can represent numbers of students, such as 2, 4, 6, 8, etc. The horizontal scale can consist of two bars. One bar represents the number of learners paid by check. The other bar represents the number of learners paid by direct deposit. The two bars can be different colors to set them apart. Bars should be the same width.

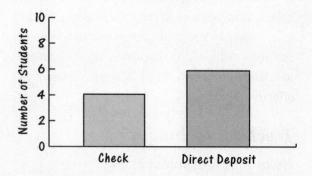

- A pie chart shows the parts that make up a whole set of facts. Each part of the pie is a percentage of the whole. For example, a pie chart might show 40% of learners are paid by check and 60% are paid by direct deposit.

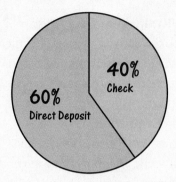

Presenting a Dialog

To present a dialog, follow these suggested steps:

- Play the tape or say the dialog aloud two or more times. Ask one or two simple questions to make sure learners understand.

- Say the dialog aloud line-by-line for learners to repeat chorally, by rows, and then individually.

- Have learners say or read the dialog together in pairs.

- Have several pairs say or read the dialog aloud for the class.

Presenting the Personal Dictionary

The Personal Dictionary enables learners to focus on the vocabulary in each unit that is relevant to their particular jobs. To use this feature, have learners work in teams to brainstorm vocabulary words they might put in their dictionaries. Have team reporters share their ideas with the class. Then allow learners a few minutes to add to their dictionaries. Remind students to continue adding words throughout the unit.

For further vocabulary development, learners can enter the words from their Personal Dictionary into their *Workforce Writing Dictionaries.*

To the Teacher

Presenting a Listening Activity

Use any of these suggestions:

- To activate learners' prior knowledge, have them look at the illustrations, if any, and say as much as they can about them. Encourage them to make inferences about the content of the listening selection.

- Have learners read the directions. To encourage them to focus their listening, have them read the questions before they listen so that they know exactly what to listen for.

- Play the tape or read the Listening Transcript aloud as learners complete the activity. Rewind the tape and play it again as necessary.

- Help learners check their work.

In multi-task listening, remind learners that they will listen to the same passage several times and answer different questions each time. After learners complete a section, have them check their own or each others' work before you rewind the tape and proceed to the next questions.

Presenting a Tip

A variety of tips throughout each unit present valuable advice on how to be a successful employee and/or language learner. To present a tip, help learners read the tip. Discuss it with them. Ask them how it will help them. For certain tips, such as those in which learners make lists, you may want to allow learners time to start the activity.

Presenting a Discussion

English ASAP provides a variety of whole-class and team discussions. Always encourage students to state their ideas and respond appropriately to other learners' comments. At the end of each discussion, have team reporters summarize their team's ideas and/or help the class come to a consensus about the topic.

Prereading

To help learners read the selections with ease and success, establish a purpose for reading and call on learners' prior knowledge to make inferences about the reading. Use any of these techniques:

◆ Have learners look over and describe any photographs, realia, and/or illustrations. Ask them to use the illustrations to say what they think the selection might be about.

◆ Have learners read the title and any heads or sub-heads. Ask them what kind of information they think is in the selection and how it might be organized. Ask them where they might encounter such information outside of class and why they would want to read it.

◆ To help learners focus their reading, have them review the comprehension activities before they read the selection. Ask them what kind of information they think they will find out when they read. Restate their ideas and/or write them on the board in acceptable English.

◆ Remind learners that they do not have to know all the words in order to understand the selection.

Evaluation

To use the Performance Check pages successfully, follow these suggested procedures:
Before and during each evaluation, create a relaxed, affirming atmosphere. Chat with the learners for a few minutes and review the material. When you and the learners are ready, have learners read the directions and look over each exercise before they complete it. If at any time you sense that learners are becoming frustrated, stop to provide additional review. Resume when learners are ready. The evaluation formats follow two basic patterns:

1. **Speaking** competencies are checked in the format used to present them in the unit. Have learners read the instructions. Make sure learners know what to do. Then have learners complete the evaluation in one of these ways:

Self- and Peer Evaluation: Have learners complete the spoken activity in pairs. Learners in each pair evaluate themselves and/or each other and report the results to you.

Teacher/Pair Evaluation: Have pairs complete the activity as you observe and evaluate their work. Begin with the most proficient learners. As other learners who are ready to be evaluated wait, have them practice in pairs. Learners who complete the evaluation successfully can peer-teach those who are waiting or those who need additional review.

Teacher/Individual Evaluation: Have individuals complete the activity with you as their partner. Follow the procedures in Teacher/Pair Evaluation.

2. **Listening, reading,** and **writing** competencies are also all checked in the same format used to present them in the unit. When learners are ready to begin, have them read the instructions. Demonstrate the first item and have learners complete the activity. In Listening activities, play the tape or read the listening transcript aloud two or more times. Then have learners check their work. Provide any review needed, and have learners try the activity again.

When learners demonstrate mastery of a skill to your satisfaction, have them record their success by checking the appropriate box in the Performance Review. The Teacher's Edition also contains charts for you to reproduce to keep track of individual and class progress.

Steck-Vaughn

English ASAP™

Connecting English to the Workplace

What do you think?

Look at the pictures.
Where do the people work?
Who are your coworkers?
Do you know their names?

Performance Preview

Can you...

☐ 1. introduce yourself?

☐ 2. make introductions?

☐ 3. complete forms for work?

Getting Started

TEAM WORK

Look at the pictures. Write the name of the language each person speaks. Write his or her job title.

I'm from Puerto Rico.

I speak _____Spanish_____ and English.

I'm a _____ .

I'm from Russia.

I speak _____Russian_____ and English.

I'm a _____ .

PRACTICE THE DIALOG

Student A chooses a picture. Student B talks about the person's country, language, and job.

A Where's she from?

B She's from Puerto Rico.

A What language does she speak?

B She speaks Spanish.

A What does she do?

B She's a mail clerk.

Now use the dialog to talk about yourself.

SURVEY

Talk to your classmates. Where are they from? Figure out what languages they speak. Do they use these languages at work? Compare information with the class.

Unit 1

 PRACTICE THE DIALOG

A Hi, I'm the new machinist.

B How are you? I'm Li Park.

A My name's Rosa Morelos.

B Did you say Rosa?

A That's right.

B Where are you from, Rosa?

A I'm from El Salvador. What about you?

B I'm from Korea.

A It's nice to meet you, Li.

B Nice to meet you, too, Rosa.

Useful Language

What languages do you speak?

I speak (Spanish) and English.

PARTNER WORK

Introduce yourself to a classmate. Tell your partner where you are from, what languages you speak, and what jobs you do. Use the dialog and Useful Language above.

ASAP
PROJECT

Make a chart with information about your class. Divide into three teams. Team 1 draws the chart and fills in the information. Team 2 asks for everyone's name and job. Team 3 asks for everyone's country and language. Look at the chart. Where do people in your class come from? Where do they work? Complete this project as you work through this unit.

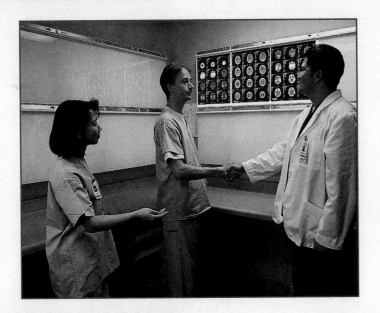

 PRACTICE THE DIALOG

A Good morning, Leon.

B Good morning, Connie.

A Leon, I'd like you to meet Marty.
Marty, this is Leon.

B It's nice to meet you, Marty.

C It's nice to meet you, too, Leon.

 Tip English speakers usually shake hands when they meet for the first time.

TEAM WORK

Work with two other students. Take turns making introductions.
Use the dialog above.

Personal Dictionary ▶ Giving Information About Yourself

Write the words and phrases that you need to know.

_____

_____

_____

 **Listening** **Knowing what to say**
....

 LISTEN AND CIRCLE

Complete the conversations. Circle the letter.

1. (a.) It's nice to meet you, too, Clark.

   b. Bye, I'll see you next week.

   c. Have a nice day.

2. a. Good morning, Jacob's Restaurant.

   b. Good evening, Jacob's Restaurant.

   c. Good afternoon, Jacob's Restaurant.

3. a. This is Pablo.

   b. It's nice to meet you, Pablo.

   c. Goodbye, Pablo.

Tip Use a greeting that's appropriate for the time of day. Before noon, say *good morning*. After noon, say *good afternoon*. After 6:00, say *good evening*.

 LISTEN AND CIRCLE

Listen to the conversations. Circle the correct information for each person.

1. Linda Marcos (mail clerk) cashier

   Eric Montoya supply room warehouse

2. Dale carpenter plumber's helper

   Martin driver foreman

3. Chen Wong China Thailand

   Marla Smith supervisor job counselor

4. Elena Rios Spanish Chinese

   Maria Santos Russian Spanish

Grammar

Learning the language you need

A. Study the Examples

I	am	from Chicago.
He	is	
She		
It		
We	are	
You		
They		

Tip Use the word *you* to refer to one person or more than one person.

COMPLETE THE SENTENCES

1. Anita __is__ a manager.

2. Carlos and Maria _____ Mexican.

3. I _____ from Korea.

4. Paolo _____ Brazilian.

5. We _____ sales assistants.

6. You _____ from El Salvador.

Tip Contractions put words together. Use an apostrophe (') to show that letters have been left out.

B. Study the Examples

I	+ am	=	I'm
He	+ is	=	He's
She	+ is	=	She's

We	+ are	=	We're
You	+ are	=	You're
They	+ are	=	They're

COMPLETE THE SENTENCES

1. I am the manager. ____I'm____ the manager of a clothing store.

2. Carlos and Maria are Mexican. _____ from Mexico City.

3. Fred and I are sales assistants. _____ sales assistants at Brand Store.

4. You are from El Salvador. _____ Central American.

5. John is a mechanic. _____ a mechanic at Auto Barn.

Talk about the people in your class or workplace.

A What does Rodolfo do?

B He's a bus driver.

A Where's he from?

B He's from Guatemala.

C. Study the Examples

I	my
he	his
she	her
it	its
we	our
you	your
they	their

My last name is Ramos.

COMPLETE THE SENTENCES

1. ___*Their*___ (Their, It's) last name is Lu.

2. _____ (His, Her) address is 56 Stanley Street.

3. _____ (His, Her) middle name is Diego.

TEAM WORK

Work with a small group. Introduce yourself. Say everyone's name.

My name is Elena.

His name is Chris.

Her name is Sylvia.

Reading and Writing

READ MAURICIO'S JOB APPLICATION

REGAL Regal Printing Company • 12 Washington Street • San Diego, CA

Fill out the form completely. Write in ink. Do not write in the box.

Name **Mauricio** **Pino**
(First) (Last)

Address **745 Glendale Drive** **San Diego** **CA** **35421**
(Number/Street) (City) (State) (Zip Code)

Telephone **(619) 555-7926**
(Area Code) (Number)

Languages **Spanish, English**

Social Security Number **000-55-7989**

Job you are applying for **typesetter**

Experience **I am an experienced typesetter.**

Do Not Write Below This Line

Interviewer's Comments _____

_____

_____

ANSWER THE QUESTIONS

1. What job is Mauricio applying for? _typesetter_____

2. What languages does he speak? _____

3. Where does Mauricio live? _____

4. What is his phone number? _____

DISCUSSION

This is the first page of the application. What other information do job applications ask for? Make a list of some things you need to know for job applications. Compare your lists.

Apply for a job at the Regal Printing Company. Follow the instructions.

REGAL Regal Printing Company • 12 Washington Street • San Diego, CA

Fill out the form completely. Write in ink. Do not write in the box.

Name _____
      (First)   (Last)

Address _____
      (Number/Street)   (City)   (State) (Zip Code)

Telephone _____
      (Area Code) (Number)

Languages _____

Social Security Number _____

Job you are applying for _____

Experience _____

_____

_____

Do Not Write Below This Line

Interviewer's Comments _____

_____

_____

typesetter

fork lift operator

mail clerk

bookkeeper

delivery driver

janitor

DISCUSSION

Look at your application carefully. Did you follow all of the instructions? Is the application complete? Is the handwriting neat? Show your application to a partner. Ask your partner if you need to make any changes.

Tip Read an entire application before you begin to fill it out. Instructions may be written at the bottom or on the back of the form.

READ THE INSURANCE FORM

Farrel Company
1200 Evans Street
Madison, WI 64441

F

Fill in the following insurance form and return to the
Human Resources Department before 12/13/99.

Name: _____Ramirez_____Ricardo_____
             (Last)   (First)

Date of Birth: _____July_____21_____1961_____
                     (Month)   (Day)   (Year)

Address: _____76 Haley Drive_____Madison_____WI____64441_____
               (Street)   (City)   (State) (Zip Code)

Telephone: _(618)_____555-9736_____
             (Area Code)   (Number)

Circle one: single   (married)   Number of Children: ____2_____

Circle the health insurance plan you want. Read the information about
each plan before you make your choice:

    Plan A   Plan B   (Plan C)

Signature: _____Ricardo Ramirez_____ Date: _12/12/99_____

ANSWER THE QUESTIONS

1. What is the name of the company? _____Farrel Company_____

2. What is the form for? _____

3. What is Ricardo's last name? _____

4. Is Ricardo married or single? _____

5. What insurance plan does Ricardo choose? _____

 *Culture Notes*

Do you fill out health insurance forms for work or school? What kinds of
information do insurance forms ask for? Are the forms hard to understand?
What is a good way to be sure your form is complete?

Performance Check

Complete the activities. Go over your work with a partner or your teacher. Then complete the Performance Review on Page 14.

SKILL 1   **INTRODUCE YOURSELF**

Introduce yourself to a classmate. Tell your partner where you are from, what languages you speak, and where you work or what jobs you do. Shake hands when you meet.

SKILL 2   **MAKE INTRODUCTIONS**

Work with two other students. Introduce one student to another. Take turns.

Unit 1

13

Fill out the job application. Check over the completed form to be sure everything is written correctly.

SUN HOTEL, MIAMI BEACH

Miami Beach, FL

555-1245

Name: _____
        (First)   (Last)

Address: _____
          (Number)   (Street)

_____
(City)   (State)   (Zip)

Telephone: _____
            (Area Code)   (Number)

Job you are applying for: _____

Experience: _____

Performance Review

I can...

☐ **1.** introduce myself.

☐ **2.** make introductions.

☐ **3.** complete forms for work.

DISCUSSION

Work with a team. How will these skills help you? Make a list. Share your list with the class.

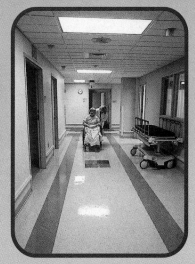

What do you think?

Look at the pictures. Name the places.

What are some other places at work?

Where do you work?

Performance Preview

Can you...

- [ ] 1. give directions to places at work?
- [ ] 2. understand directions to places at work?
- [ ] 3. name places at work?
- [ ] 4. use a to-do list?

TEAM WORK

Match the word with the picture. Share your answers with the class.

a. break room

b. entrance

c. exit

d. hall

e. meeting room

f. office

g. parking lot

h. rest rooms

i. supply room

PARTNER WORK

Student A points to a picture. Student B says the place.

ON YOUR JOB SURVEY

Look at the places. Which ones are at your workplace or school?
Circle the letters. Then work with a partner. Compare your lists.
Which places did you both circle?

Talk About It

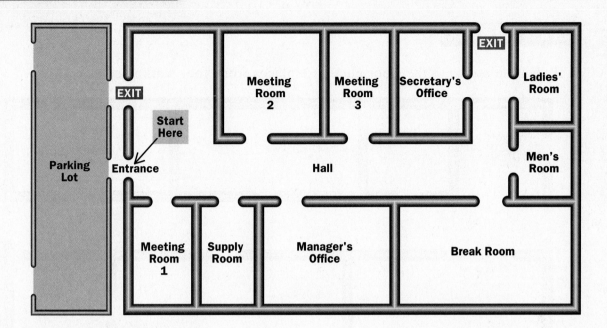

PRACTICE THE DIALOG

A Please take this package to the supply room.

B Where's the supply room?

A Go down the hall. It's the second door on the right.

B Excuse me. Is it the first door on the right?

A No, it's the second door on the right. It's next to the manager's office.

B Thanks.

PARTNER WORK

Ask your partner for directions. Use the map. Use the dialog and the Useful Language above.

Useful Language

Go down the hall.

Turn left/right.

It's the first/second/third/fourth door on the right.

It's next to the supply room.

It's between the men's room and the exit.

It's across the hall from the supply room.

ASAP PROJECT

As a class, prepare a floor plan of your workplace or school. Divide into three teams. One team gets the information. Another team draws the floor plan. Another team writes questions about the floor plan for the class to answer.

Keep Talking

Asking for and giving directions

 PARTNER WORK

Label the rooms in the floor plan. Use places from your workplace or school.

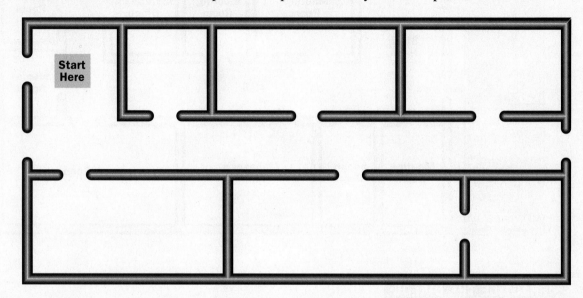

Start Here

 PRACTICE THE DIALOG

Student A asks for directions.
Student B gives directions.

A Where's _____ ?

B _____

A Excuse me. Is it next to _____ ?

B Yes, it is./No, it isn't. It's next to _____ .

A Thanks.

 Tip To learn the names of places, start a list of the places you go to at work and the things you get or do there.

supply room—get pens

Personal Dictionary ⟩ Giving Directions

Write the words and phrases that you need to know.

_____

_____

_____

Unit 2

Listening

Listening to directions

LISTEN AND CIRCLE

Circle the places you hear.

Exit	(**Kitchen**)	**Meeting Room 1**
Meeting Room 2	**Meeting Room 3**	**Meeting Room 4**
Men's Room	**Office**	**Parking Lot**
Supply Room	**Telephones**	**Ladies' Room**

LISTEN AGAIN

Write the name of the room on the floor plan.

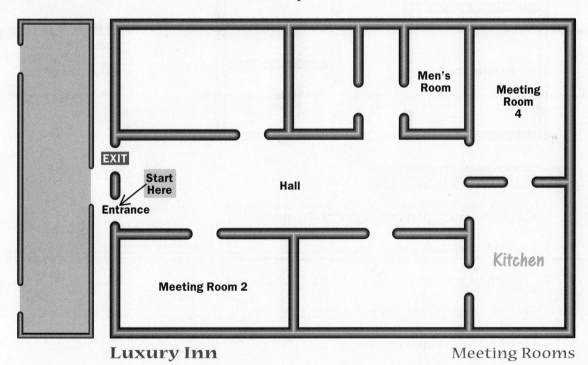

Luxury Inn   Meeting Rooms

Grammar

A. Study the Examples

Am	I	in the hall?
Is	he	
	she	
	it	
Are	we	
	you	
	they	

Yes,	I	am.
	he	is.
	she	
	it	
	we	are.
	you	
	they	

No,	I'm	not.
	he	isn't.
	she	
	it	
	we	aren't.
	you	
	they	

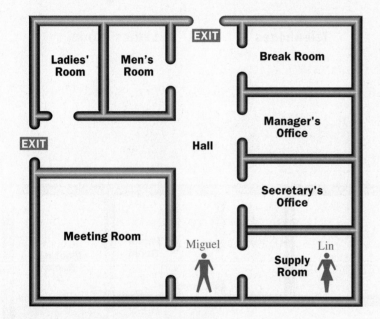

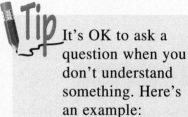

Tip It's OK to ask a question when you don't understand something. Here's an example:

Excuse me. Is the supply room next to the exit?

ANSWER THE QUESTIONS

Look at the floor plan and answer the questions.

1. Are Miguel and Lin at home? _____ *No, they aren't.* _____

2. Are they at work? _____

3. Is Lin in the break room? _____

4. Is she in the supply room? _____

5. Is Miguel in the hall? _____

6. Is the meeting room next to the break room? _____

Unit 2

B. Study the Examples

Where's	the exit?
	the supply room?

The exit is	down the hall.
	across the hall from the rest rooms.
	next to the break room.
	between the break room and the men's room.

TEAM WORK

Talk about places at your workplace or school.

A Where's _____?

B It's _____.

A Is it next to _____?

B Yes, it is./No, it isn't. It's _____.

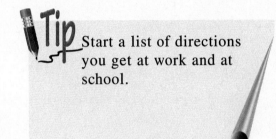

Tip Start a list of directions you get at work and at school.

C. Study the Examples

Go	down the hall.
	to the supply room.

COMPLETE THE DIRECTIONS

Look at the floor plan on page 20. Tell Lin how to get to the rest room.
Write the verb on the line.

Go	Turn	Turn	Walk

1. _Go_ out the door.

2. _____ right.

3. _____ down the hall.

4. _____ left. The rest room is on the right.

TEAM WORK

Write directions you get at work or school. Then write directions you give.
Share your directions with the class.

Reading and Writing

READ ANA'S TO-DO LIST

TO DO

1. Go to computer class.
2. Get supplies from the supply room.
3. Make photocopies.
4. Take letters to Mr. Green's office.

WRITE THE NUMBER

What does Ana need to do first? Second? Third? Write numbers from 1 to 3.

DISCUSSION

Ana doesn't have time to do one thing on her list. Circle the number in the list. What does Ana tell her boss? Share your ideas with the class.

Your team is cleaning your classroom or workplace. Write a to-do list. Share your list with the class.

TO DO

Useful Language

buy   clean   get

meet   put   take

WRITE A TO-DO LIST

What do you need to do? Write a to-do list for work, home, or school.

DISCUSSION

Work with a team. Talk about to-do lists. What kind of to-do list do you make for going shopping? Going to the doctor? Planning a trip? Share your ideas with the class.

Extension Reading a building directory

DIRECTORY		15 GREEN STREET	
	Suite		**Suite**
Computer Training		Reliable Home Health Care	
Associates	400	Human Resources	100
		Visiting Nurses' Office	150
Mexicali Foods Co.		Lab	Basement
Executive Offices	200		
Human Resources	210	Dr. Anita Thomas, D.D.S.	160
Sales	300		
Customer Service	350		

ANSWER THE QUESTIONS

Where do they go? Write the suite number.

1. Miguel's taking a package to the sales department of Mexicali Foods. Suite _300_

2. Alicia's taking a computer class. Suite _____

3. Leo wants a job at Reliable Home Health Care. Suite _____

4. Sara has an appointment with Dr. Thomas. Suite _____

5. You want a job at Mexicali Foods. Suite _____

CultureNotes

When you need directions at work or at school, who do you ask? Why? If you don't understand the directions, what do you do? Why?

Performance Check

Complete the activities. Go over your work with a partner or your teacher. Then complete the Performance Review on page 26.

SKILL 1 GIVE DIRECTIONS

Give your partner or teacher directions to the Manager's Office.

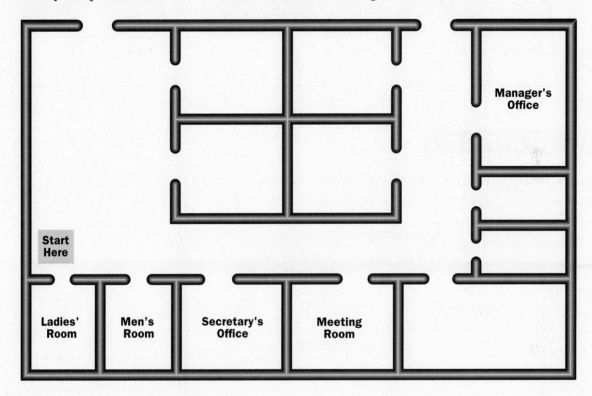

SKILL 2 UNDERSTAND DIRECTIONS

Listen and write the name of the room on the floor plan.

| Break Room | Supply Room |

Unit 2

Write the name of the place on the line.

break room	hall	office	supply room

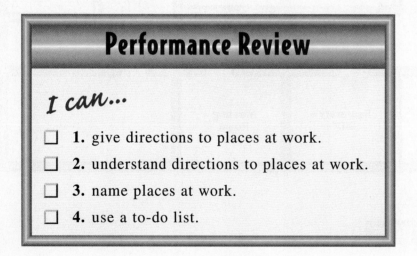

_____   _____   _____

What do you need to do tomorrow? Write a to-do list on a sheet of paper.

Performance Review

I can...

- ☐ **1.** give directions to places at work.
- ☐ **2.** understand directions to places at work.
- ☐ **3.** name places at work.
- ☐ **4.** use a to-do list.

DISCUSSION

Work with a team. How will your new skills help you? Make a list. Share your list with the class.

What do you think?

Look at the pictures.

Name the machines the people are using.

What machines can you use?

Can you teach others to use them?

Performance Preview

Can you...

☐ 1. listen to and follow instructions?

☐ 2. set up and use a machine?

☐ 3. read a diagram?

☐ 4. explain how to use a machine?

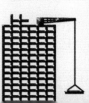

Getting Started

TEAM WORK

Anton is working in the mailroom. Work with your team. Find all the machines Anton uses. Write the names of the machines. Talk about what each machine does.

fax machine

_____   _____

_____   _____

_____   _____

_____   _____

PARTNER WORK

Look at the machines Anton uses. Student A chooses a machine.
Student B says what Anton can do with it.

A the computer

B Anton can write a letter on the computer.

SURVEY

As a class, make a chart with three columns: home, work, and school.
Each person writes the name of a machine he or she uses at each place.

Unit 3

Talk About It

 PRACTICE THE DIALOG

A Do you need some help?

B Yes, I'm trying to copy this memo.

A First, open the cover and put the paper on the glass.

B Like this?

A That's right. Then, choose the number of copies you want. Next, close the cover and press the START button.

B Thanks for your help.

Useful Language

turn on	**first**
turn off	**second**
open	**third**
close	**next**
plug in	**last**

 PARTNER WORK

Make a list of machines people use at work or at home. Use the dialog and the Useful Language above to talk about how you operate these machines. What do you do if you need help?

ASAP PROJECT

As a class, choose a machine from work or home. Form three teams. One team makes a list of instructions for using the machine. Another team draws simple diagrams. The third team makes a poster of the instructions and the diagrams. Complete this project as you work through this unit.

Showing someone how to use a machine

Talk about what each person is doing.
Choose a machine for each person.

___b___ 1. Anita is cleaning.

_____ 2. Sumiko is ringing up a sale.

_____ 3. Donna is building a bookcase.

_____ 4. Luis is starting work.

 PRACTICE THE DIALOG

Choose a machine from the pictures. Tell your partner how to use the machine.
Student A asks for instructions. Student B gives instructions.

A How do you use the coffee maker?

B First, put in the water. Next, put in the coffee.

A First water, then coffee?

B That's right. Now turn it on.

A Thanks for your help.

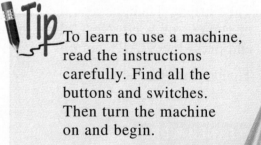

Tip To learn to use a machine, read the instructions carefully. Find all the buttons and switches. Then turn the machine on and begin.

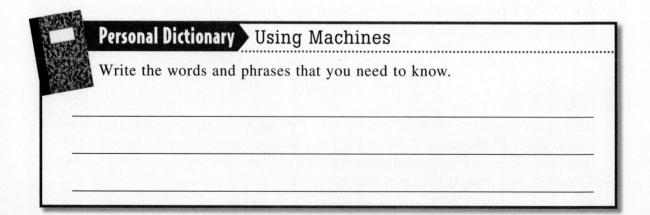

Personal Dictionary Using Machines

Write the words and phrases that you need to know.

_____

_____

_____

Unit 3

Following steps in order ······························

 LISTEN AND NUMBER

Listen to the instructions. Number the machine's parts in the order you use them.

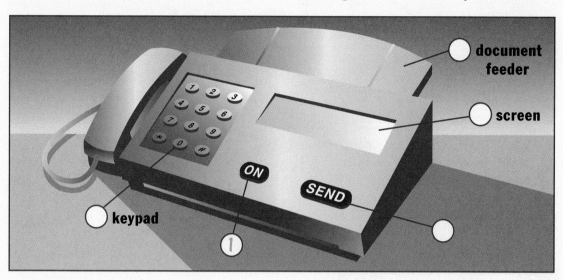

LISTEN AND NUMBER

Number the steps in the correct order.

Unit 3

Grammar

A. Study the Examples

I'm	reading the instructions.
He's	
She's	
We're	
You're	
They're	

I'm not		reading the instructions.
He	isn't	
She		
We	aren't	
You		
They		

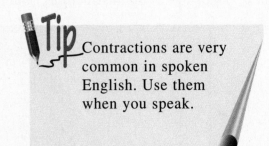

Tip Contractions are very common in spoken English. Use them when you speak.

COMPLETE THE SENTENCES

Use the language in A.

1. Hong _'s calling_____ (**call**) her supervisor.

2. We _____ (**take**) a computer class on Monday.

3. Oscar _____ (**not work**) today.

4. They _____ (**not clean**) the office now.

5. They _____ (**work**) on another floor.

6. I _____ (**not start**) work late.

B. Study the Examples

Am	I	pushing the right button?
Is	he	
	she	
Are	we	
	you	
	they	

Yes,	you	are.
No,		aren't.

What	are you	doing?
Where		going?

Nina is taking a training class at work. Use the language in A and B.

A Where _____are_____ you _____going_____ (**go**), Nina?

B I_____ (**go**) to the training room.

A _____ you _____ (**take**) a class?

B Yes, I _____ .

A What _____ they _____ (**teach**)?

B They_____ (**teach**) me to use the new press.

PARTNER WORK

Does your company have training classes? Are you taking a training class? What are you learning?

C. Study the Examples

the mail supervisor's desk

the employees' cars

WRITE THE ANSWER

Who does it belong to? Follow the language in C.

1. the secretary—telephone

_____the secretary's telephone_____

2. Bruno—adding machine

_____

3. the cashiers—keys

_____

4. the tailor—sewing machine

_____

Unit 3

TEAM WORK

Label the parts of the vacuum cleaner.

plug	ON/OFF switch	cover	bag

plug

PARTNER WORK

Talk about the questions. Share your answers with the class.

1. What's this machine for?

2. Where is the plug?

3. Where do you put the bag in?

4. How do you turn the machine on?

 **DISCUSSION**

Think of a machine you know how to use. Does it have a diagram or instructions? How does a diagram help you learn to use the machine? Where do you find the diagram and instructions?

Your supervisor wants you to help your coworkers with the new vacuum cleaner. Look at the diagram. Write the steps for putting in the bag and using the vacuum cleaner.

Vacuum Cleaner Instructions

1. Open the cover.

2.

3.

4.

5.

open

close

put

press

switch

DISCUSSION

Look at another team's instructions. Are they different from yours? How are they different? What makes some instructions easy to follow and some instructions difficult? How can you make your instructions for using the vacuum cleaner better?

READ THE INSTRUCTIONS

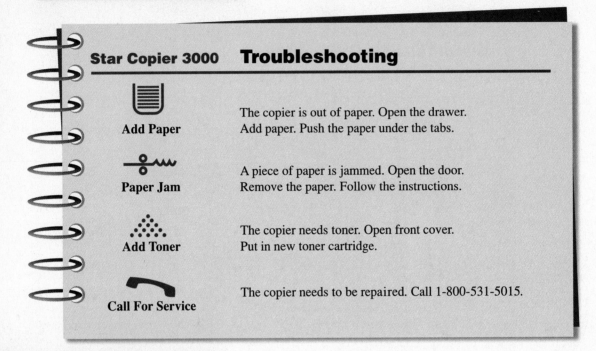

Star Copier 3000   Troubleshooting

Add Paper

The copier is out of paper. Open the drawer.
Add paper. Push the paper under the tabs.

Paper Jam

A piece of paper is jammed. Open the door.
Remove the paper. Follow the instructions.

Add Toner

The copier needs toner. Open front cover.
Put in new toner cartridge.

Call For Service

The copier needs to be repaired. Call 1-800-531-5015.

 PRACTICE THE DIALOG

Practice the dialog. Then use the dialog to say
what you should do if other lights are flashing.

A What's wrong?

B The copier isn't working. One of the lights is flashing.

A You're right. That's the toner light flashing.

B What should I do?

A Open the cover and put in a new toner cartridge.

B Thanks.

 *Culture Notes*

What can go wrong when you are using a machine? Do you ask for help?
Who do you ask? Where else can you find help?

Performance Check

Complete the activities. Go over your work with a partner or your teacher.
Then complete the Performance Review on Page 38.

SKILL 1 **FOLLOW INSTRUCTIONS**

Listen to the instructions for putting paper in the copier.
Number the steps in the correct order.

_____ Open the top paper drawer.

_____ Push the paper under the tabs.

_____ Close the drawer.

_____ Press the red button.

_____ Put the paper in the drawer.

SKILL 2 **SET UP AND USE A MACHINE**

Read the instructions for the coffee maker.
Then write *yes* or *no*.

Is this what you do?

_____ **1.** Plug in the coffee maker first.

_____ **2.** Put water into the filter basket.

_____ **3.** Pour water into the water tank.

_____ **4.** Press the READY button to start the machine.

_____ **5.** After you put in the water and coffee, press the ON button.

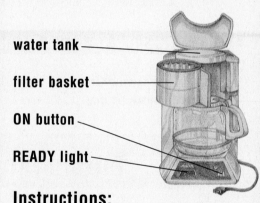

water tank

filter basket

ON button

READY light

Instructions:

1. Put coffee into the filter basket.

2. Pour water into the water tank.

3. Plug in the coffee maker.

4. Press the ON button.

5. Coffee is ready when the READY light comes on.

Unit 3

Look at the diagram of a cash register. Write the letter.

_____ **1.** You keep money here.   **a.** screen

_____ **2.** You use this to turn it on.   **b.** keypad

_____ **3.** You use this to enter the prices.   **c.** cash drawer

_____ **4.** You see the prices here.   **d.** ON key

SKILL 4 **EXPLAIN HOW TO USE A MACHINE**

Think of a machine you know how to use. Tell your partner or your teacher how to use it.

Performance Review

I can...

☐ **1.** listen to and follow instructions.

☐ **2.** set up and use a machine.

☐ **3.** read a diagram.

☐ **4.** explain how to use a machine.

Discussion

Work with a team. How will the skills help you? Make a list.
Share your list with the class.

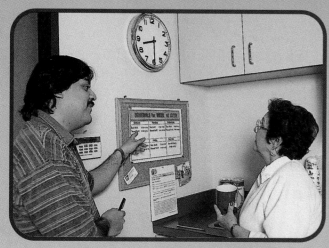

What do you think?

Look at the pictures.

What are the people doing?

What time do you go to work?

Do you work full time or part time?

Are you looking for a job?

Performance Preview

Can you...

- ☐ 1. read, write, and say times, days, and dates?
- ☐ 2. interpret work schedules?
- ☐ 3. ask to change your work hours?
- ☐ 4. respond to schedule changes?

Getting Started

Telling time

TEAM WORK

Look at the clocks. Say what time it is. What are you doing at these times?
What are your classmates doing?

PARTNER WORK

Student A asks what time it is. Student B answers.
Follow the dialog below.

A What time is it?

B It's 3:30.

SURVEY

Sylvia works full time. She works 40 hours per week. Talk to your classmates.
Do they work part time or full time? How many hours do they work in a week?
Make a list.

Sylvia	full time	40 hours

Unit 4

Reading times and dates

PRACTICE THE DIALOG

A What's the date next Thursday?

B Next Thursday is June 20.

A Are you sure? I'd like to take that day off.

B Why?

A I have to take my commercial driver's license test.

B You'd better talk to the manager right away.

What day would you like to take off? Talk to your partner.
Use the dialog above.

PARTNER WORK

Look at Sara's calendar. Answer the questions.

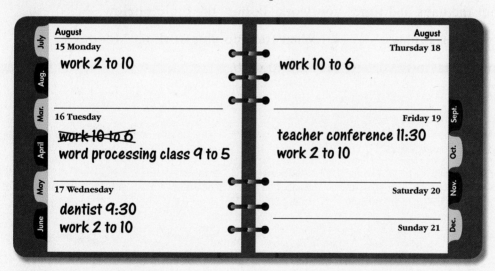

1. What month is it?

2. Does Sara work on Wednesday?

3. What days does Sara work from 2 to 10?

ASAP
PROJECT

Everyone in the class works for the Copy Shop. The Copy Shop is open from 10:00 in the morning to 10:00 at night every day. Make a work schedule for everyone in the class. People can work full time or part time. Put break times on the schedule. Complete this project as you work through this unit.

Keep Talking

Changing your schedule

PRACTICE THE DIALOG

Raymundo wants to leave early. Ms. Kelly is his supervisor.

A Ms. Kelly, can I leave early on Tuesday? I have an appointment with my son's teacher.

B What time do you want to leave?

A 2:30.

B Yes, that's fine.

A Thank you, Ms. Kelly.

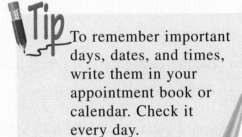

Tip To remember important days, dates, and times, write them in your appointment book or calendar. Check it every day.

PARTNER WORK

You work at Bright Cleaning Services. Look at the schedule. Take turns talking. Talk about the days and times you work. Follow the dialog below.

A Do you work on Friday?

B No, I have Friday off.

A What time do you work on Monday?

B 8:30 to 4:30.

Bright Cleaning Service

Schedule for week of 7/17 to 7/22

	Monday	Tuesday	Wednesday	Thursday	Friday	Saturday
	8:30-4:30	8:30-4:30	10:00-6:00	2:00-10:00	Off	10:00-1:00
Lunch	12:30-1:30	12:30-1:30	1:00-2:00			

Personal Dictionary ▶ Time, Calendars, Schedules

Write the words and phrases that you need to know.

_____

_____

_____

Unit 4

 LISTEN AND CIRCLE

Listen and circle the times you hear.

1. (7:30)   9:45   10:25
2. 7:00   11:00   11:30
3. 10:20   10:50   12:45
4. 4:05   4:15   4:45
5. 10:15   10:30   10:50

 LISTEN AND WRITE

Listen and write Nora's work schedule on the calendar.

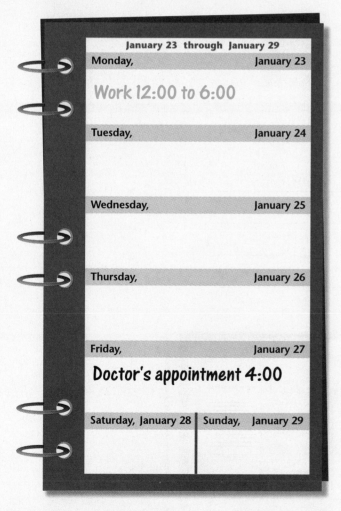

January 23 through January 29	
Monday,	**January 23**
Work 12:00 to 6:00	
Tuesday,	**January 24**
Wednesday,	**January 25**
Thursday,	**January 26**
Friday,	**January 27**
Doctor's appointment 4:00	
Saturday, January 28	**Sunday, January 29**

 Tip

Say the numbers 13 and 30. Your voice goes up on the thir<u>teen</u>. Your voice goes down on the <u>thir</u>t<u>y</u>. Can you hear the difference? Practice saying these numbers.

14, 40   15, 50   16, 60
17, 70   18, 80   19, 90

A. Study the Examples

Can	I	leave work early today?
	you	
	he	
	she	
	we	
	they	

Yes,	I	can.
No,	you	can't.
	he	
	she	
	we	
	they	

PARTNER WORK

Take turns asking to leave work early. Answer the request.

B. Study the Examples

What	time	is it?
	month	
	day	
	year	

It's	7:15.
	January.
	Tuesday.
	2001.

ANSWER THE QUESTIONS

Look at the picture.

1. What time is it? _____It's 3:45._____

2. What day is it? _____

3. What month is it? _____

4. What year is it? _____

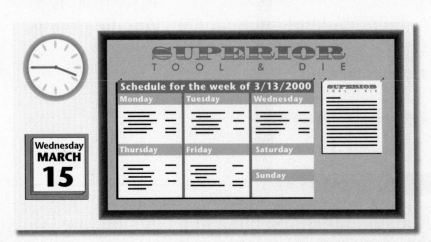

C. Study the Examples

Is it	Tuesday?
	July 15?
	3:00?
	Memorial Day?

Yes,	it	is.
No,		isn't.

COMPLETE THE DIALOGS

Look at the calendar. Complete the sentences.

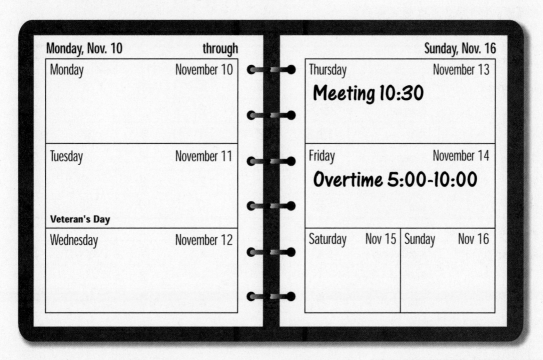

1. **A** Do you work tomorrow?

   B Is tomorrow Tuesday?

   A Yes, _it is_ .

   B No, I'm not working.

   A Why?

   B _____ Veteran's Day. _____ a holiday.

2. **A** _____ time for the meeting?

   B No, it _____ . The meeting is at 10:30.

   A What time _____ now?

   B _____ 9:45.

PARTNER WORK

Look at the calendar. Today is Friday. What's the date? What's on the calendar? What's on your calendar today?

Reading and Writing

READ THE WORK SCHEDULE

Figure out the total number of hours each person works. Remember to include overtime. Write the numbers in the last column.

SUPERIOR TOOL & DIE

Schedule for the week of 3/13/2000

First shift 7:30-3:30		Monday 3/13	Tuesday 3/14	Wednesday 3/15	Thursday 3/16	Friday 3/17	Total Hours
J. Ramirez	Regular hours	8	8	8	8	8	40
	Overtime	5.5		3			8.5
	Total	13.5	8	11	8	8	
S. Faldo	Regular hours	8	Day Off	8	8	8	32
	Overtime			2	2	3	7
	Total	8	0	10	10	11	
Second shift 2:00-10:00							
N. Malnoff	Regular hours	8	8	8	8	Day Off	32
	Overtime	1			2		3
	Total	9	8	8	10	0	

ANSWER THE QUESTIONS

Write *yes* or *no*.

1. It's Tuesday. Is Joe Ramirez working first shift? <u>yes</u>

2. Does Sara Faldo have Wednesday off? _____

3. Is Thursday the 19? _____

4. It's Thursday. Is Natalie Malnoff working overtime? _____

DISCUSSION

Joe Ramirez has a doctor's appointment on Tuesday at 3:00. What can he do? Who should he speak to? Who do you speak to if you need to leave early or come in late to work?

You work at Superior Tool & Die Co. You have the same schedule as Sara Faldo. Write your schedule for this week.

SUPERIOR
T O O L & D I E

Work Schedule for the week of _____

Name _____	Monday	Tuesday	Wednesday	Thursday	Friday	Total Hours
Regular hours	8					
Overtime						
Total						

PARTNER WORK

Write your own schedule for work or school. Use the blank form.
Compare your schedule to your partner's. Do you have the same hours?
Do you both take breaks? Do you work overtime?

Work Schedule for the week of _____

Name _____	Monday	Tuesday	Wednesday	Thursday	Friday	Total Hours
Regular hours						
Overtime						
Total						

DISCUSSION

Is your work schedule the same every week? Do you write it down?
How does writing down your schedule help you plan your time better?

Extension · · · **Asking for time off** · · · · · · · · · ·

FILL IN THE FORM

You want to take half the day off on Friday, October 16, to go to a conference with your child's teacher. Fill in the form. Include your name and the date.

Request for Time Off Report

Name _____   Date _____

Reason for absence	Dates			
☐ Vacation	From____ To____	No. of days ____	No. of hours ____
☐ Sick	From____ To____	No. of days ____	No. of hours ____
☑ Personal	From____ To____	No. of days ____	No. of hours ____
☐ Death in family	From____ To____	No. of days ____	No. of hours ____
☐ Accident on Job	From____ To____	No. of days ____	No. of hours ____
☐ Other	From____ To____	No. of days ____	No. of hours ____

Explanation (if necessary) _____

_____

_____

Supervisor's approval _____ Date _____

Please forward to Office Coordinator after Supervisor has signed.

ANSWER THE QUESTIONS

1. Who signs the form?

2. What do you think personal days are for?

 *Culture Notes*

Information about days off, sick days, and overtime is often in the employee handbook. Do you have an employee handbook where you work? Who do you ask if you want time off? Do you have to fill out a form?

Unit 4

How well can you use skills in this unit?

Complete the activities. Go over your work with a partner or your teacher. Then complete the Performance Review on page 50.

SKILL 1   READ, WRITE, AND SAY TIMES, DAYS, AND DATES

Look at the clocks. Say and write what time it is.

_____   _____   _____   _____

SKILL 2   INTERPRET WORK SCHEDULES

VALDEZ CLEANING SERVICES   Schedule for the week of 2/14/2000

		Monday 2/14	Tuesday 2/15	Wednesday 2/16	Thursday 2/17	Friday 2/18	Total Hours
First shift 7:00-3:00							
S. Hernandez	Regular hours	8	8	8	off	8	32
	Overtime	7					7
	Total	15	8	8		8	39
Second shift 2:00-10:00							
V. Toshi	Regular hours	8	off	8	8	8	32
	Overtime					3	3
	Total	8		8	8	11	35

Read the schedule. Answer the questions.

1. Who works first shift? _____

2. What day does Sandra Hernandez have off? _____

3. When did Sandra Hernandez work overtime? _____

4. How many hours did Victor Toshi work overtime? _____

You work Monday through Friday from 9:00 to 5:00. Look below at your personal calendar for next week. When do you need to change your work hours? Your partner or your teacher is your supervisor. Ask to change your work hours. Remember to say why.

Sunday	Monday	Tuesday	Wednesday	Thursday	Friday	Saturday
4	5	6	7	8	9	10
	9-dentist			5:45 pick up Sam		party for Mom

SKILL 4   RESPOND TO SCHEDULE CHANGES

Look at the weekly schedule again. Your supervisor asks you to make some changes to your regular schedule. Answer *yes* or *no*. Say why you can or cannot make the changes. Follow the dialog below.

A Can you stay late on Thursday?

B No, I'm sorry. I have to pick up my son Sam at day care after work.

Performance Review

I can...

☐ **1.** read, write, and say times, days, and dates.

☐ **2.** interpret work schedules.

☐ **3.** ask to change my work hours.

☐ **4.** respond to schedule changes.

DISCUSSION

Work with a team. How will the skills help you? Make a list. Share your list with the class.

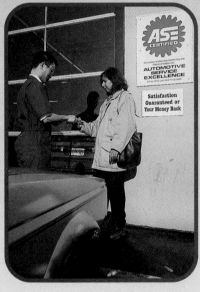

What Do You Think?

Look at the pictures.

Do you think the customer service is good?

Do you talk to customers at work?

How do you help them?

Performance Preview

Can you...

☐ 1. greet customers?

☐ 2. give good customer service?

☐ 3. understand commitments to customers?

☐ 4. respond to customers' complaints?

Getting Started

TEAM WORK

Look at the pictures. Each employee is greeting a customer.
What is each employee saying? Write the letter.

a. Thank you for calling the National
Catalog Company. May I take your order?

b. Good morning. Can I get you some
coffee or juice?

c. Hello. Can I help you with your bags?
Where are you flying to today?

d. Welcome to Ace Electronics.
Can I show you anything special?

PARTNER WORK

List different businesses and ways they greet customers.
Then take turns greeting customers. Follow the example.

Welcome to Antonio's Restaurant. How many in your group?

SURVEY

What is a polite way to say hello to a new customer? Talk to your classmates.
Make a list of greetings. Label one list *very polite*, the second list *polite*, and
the third list *less polite*.

Unit 5

PRACTICE THE DIALOG

A Good morning. May I help you?

B Yes, I'd like to return this camera. It's broken.

A No problem. Would you like a refund or an exchange?

B I'd like a refund, please.

Discussion

How does the sales associate in the dialog give good customer service? Think of a time when you returned something to a store. Was the service good or bad? Why?

PARTNER WORK

Use the dialog above and the Useful Language. Practice giving good customer service in these situations:

1. You are a waiter. Some customers don't like their table. They want a different table.

2. You are an airline reservations agent. A passenger would like a different seat on the plane.

Useful Language

Hello/Hi.

How can I help you?

Of course.

Sure/Fine.

ASAP PROJECT

As a class, prepare a list of customer service DOs and DON'Ts. Divide into two teams. One team makes the list of DOs. The other team makes the list of DON'Ts. Review the lists as a class. Complete this project as you work through this unit.

Keep Talking

Apologizing to customers

PRACTICE THE DIALOG

A City Roofing. May I help you?

B Yes, this is Sara Jones. I'm having a problem with my new roof.

A I'm sorry, Ms. Jones. What's the problem?

B It's leaking again. Can you send someone out to fix it?

A Sure. I'll send someone out later today. What's your address?

B 13 Evergreen Street in Middletown. Thanks for your help.

Useful Language

I apologize.

Please accept our apology.

Can I offer you a refund/ exchange/discount?

We'll take care of the problem.

PARTNER WORK

Look at the pictures. Your partner is the customer who has a problem. You try to help by giving good customer service and by apologizing. Use the dialog and the Useful Language above.

Personal Dictionary Serving Customers

Write the words and phrases that you need to know.

_____

_____

_____

Unit 5

LISTEN AND WRITE

Listen to the orders. Write the number of items the customer says.

1. __12__ rolls of tape

2. _____ monitors, _____ keyboards

3. _____ gallons of off-white paint, _____ gallons of dark green paint

4. _____ envelopes, _____ boxes

 LISTEN AND WRITE

Listen to the customer place an order. Write the number of each item the customer wants.

THRIFTY
ELECTRICAL SUPPLY

Date: **5/17/99**   Order Number: **23–56783**

Name: **Georgia Bard**

Telephone: **555-6234**

Address: **17 Nobel Road**

Los Angeles, CA 90027

Qty.	Description	Price for each	Total
3	boxes light bulbs	$1.95	$ 5.85
	switches	$7.95	
	extension cords	$2.50	
	plugs	$3.95	

 Tip

Double-check the information when you talk to a customer. Ask the customer to repeat each item. Then, read the information back to the customer to make sure it is exactly right.

Did you say...?
Can you repeat that, please?
Was that...?

 LISTEN AGAIN

Listen again and write the total cost for each item on the form.

A. Study the Examples

I need	a	tube of glue.
	an	electric drill.
	some	nails and screws.

I need	some	glue.
		paint.

COMPLETE THE DIALOG

Look at the sales flier for Jiffy Auto Supplies. Complete the dialog.
Use *a/an* or *some*.

A Do you have any oil filters?

B Yes, we have _____some_____ oil filters on sale this week.

A Good. I'd like _____ oil filter.

B OK, do you need _____ oil, too?

A Yes. I'd also like _____ package of spark plugs.

B Is there anything else?

A Just _____ windshield washer fluid.

B Oh, I'm sorry. We don't have any windshield washer fluid left.

B. Study the Examples

How	much	gas	do you want?
		oil	
	many	gallons of gas	
		batteries	

WRITE THE QUESTION

You are a sales associate at Jiffy Auto Supplies. Find out what your customer needs. Write questions with *How much* or *How many*.

1. spark plugs

                How many spark plugs do you need?

2. oil filters

_____

3. oil

_____

4. windshield washer fluid

_____

5. brake pads

_____

TEAM WORK

Make a list of office supplies you use at work, home, or school. Find out how much or how many of each item people use. Fill out the supply request form.

REQUESTS FOR SUPPLIES

All supplies must be approved by the office manager.

Department Number: **23-4567**   Date: **June 2, 1999**

Order:	Item	Quantity
	pencils	*1 box*
	_____	_____
	_____	_____

Manager's Signature: _____

READ THE CUSTOMER SERVICE POLICY

Discount Office Products

CUSTOMER SERVICE POLICY

1. Any item with a receipt can be returned for a full refund or exchange.

2. Items returned without a receipt can be returned for a store credit.

3. Telephone orders are guaranteed to arrive in 1 day.

4. The Customer Service Department is open 24 hours a day. Call 555-2323.

WRITE THE NUMBER

You work at Discount Office Products. Read each situation.
Write the number of the policy.

___4___ 1. Maria's supervisor wants her to order some computer disks. It's 5:30.

_____ 2. Universal Trucking ordered five boxes of copier paper on July 13. It's July 16 and the paper has not arrived.

_____ 3. Tim bought an electric pencil sharpener. It doesn't work. He still has his receipt.

_____ 4. The assistant manager of Cafe America wants to return a broken stapler. She doesn't have her receipt.

DISCUSSION

Is there a customer service policy where you work? What happens if a customer is not satisfied with the service? What does your supervisor want you to do? Do customers know what the customer service policy is? How do they know?

READ THE MAINTENANCE REQUEST

The people in your workplace can also be your customers. To give them good service you do your work quickly and well. For example, imagine you are a maintenance worker at Brown Company. A coworker sent you this maintenance request. What do you do first? Second? Third? Number the problems from 1 to 3.

BROWN COMPANY
Maintenance Request

Name: **Sonia Valdez**   Date: **12/1**

Department: **Shipping**

Problem: **The lights aren't working in the supply room.**   1

Problem: **A chair in the break room is broken.**

Problem: **The lock on the exit door doesn't work.**

Please describe each problem.
All repairs will be made within two days of receiving the request.

WRITE A MAINTENANCE REQUEST

Think about your workplace or school. List three problems that you want to report to the maintenance department. Complete the form.

Maintenance Request

Name: _____   Date: _____

Department: _____

Problem: _____

Problem: _____

Problem: _____

Please describe each problem.
All repairs will be made within two days of receiving the request.

DISCUSSION

A chef in a restaurant can give good customer service to the waiters.
The chef prepares the food quickly and well, and then the waiters are happy.
Who do you give good customer service to at work or at school? How?

Unit 5   59

READ THE CUSTOMER SERVICE CARD

Holiday Hotels

How was our service?
Please let us know how we can serve you better.

Name: __S. Aziz__   Phone Number: __555-9070__ Date: __5/6/99__

Circle the number after each statement.

Statement	agree				disagree
Checking in and out is fast and efficient.	1	2	③	4	5
My room was neat and clean.	1	2	3	④	5
The staff is friendly and helpful.	1	②	3	4	5
Room service is delivered quickly.	1	2	3	4	⑤

Comments: __The room was not clean when I arrived. I waited over
45 minutes for my food from room service.__

ANSWER THE QUESTIONS

1. Does Mr. Aziz have any complaints?

2. What are his complaints?

3. What does Mr. Aziz think of the service?

4. Do you think Mr. Aziz is a satisfied customer? Why or why not?

PARTNER WORK

You are assistant hotel managers. Make a list of things you can do
to help make Mr. Aziz happy and keep him as a customer. Share your
list with the class.

ON YOUR JOB Culture Notes

Service can be bad for many reasons. What can you do if a coworker gives
poor service? Talk about ways to help employees to give better service.

Complete the activities. Go over your work with a partner or your teacher. Then complete the Performance Review on page 62.

SKILL 1 **GREET CUSTOMERS**

Work with a partner. Imagine a customer at this gas station or at a job you would like to have. Greet him or her.

SKILL 2 **GIVE GOOD CUSTOMER SERVICE**

Work with your partner or teacher. He or she complains. You give good customer service. Find out what the problem is and offer a solution.

You work for Superior Heating and Air Conditioning. Look at its customer service policies. Then talk about the situations. What do the policies say should happen? Tell your partner or your teacher.

SUPERIOR
Heating and Air Conditioning

1. All work is guaranteed.

2. Service technicians must arrive on time. If a technician is more than 10 minutes late, there is a 15% discount.

3. We match all competitors' prices.

1. Mr. Rodriguez's air conditioner isn't working. It is 11:15. The service technician is 30 minutes late.

2. Helen Lin has a new water heater. It is leaking on the floor. She calls to complain.

SKILL 4 **RESPOND TO CUSTOMERS' COMPLAINTS**

Look at Skill 3. Apologize to the customers for the mistakes. Work with your partner or teacher.

Performance Review

I can...

☐ 1. greet customers.

☐ 2. give good customer service.

☐ 3. understand commitments to customers.

☐ 4. respond to customers' complaints.

DISCUSSION

Work with a team. How will the skills help you? Make a list. Share the list with your class.

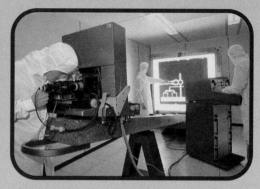

What Do You Think?

Look at the pictures.

Where are they working?

Are they dressed appropriately?

Are they following the rules?

Are there rules at your workplace?

Performance Preview

Can you...

☐ 1. follow company rules?

☐ 2. call in sick?

☐ 3. use polite language?

☐ 4. improve your performance?

TEAM WORK

Read the sentences. Talk about each person's job. What do you think each person wears to work? Write the letters.

a. sweatshirt

b. hat

c. coveralls

d. work boots

1. Sylvia's a welder at Quality Fabricators. _a, d_

2. Marisol's a bus driver for City Bus Line. _____

3. Mark's a plumber at Quick Plumbing Company. _____

4. Betty's a carpenter at Triangle Builders. _____

PRACTICE THE DIALOG

Dawn just started at Best Electric. Mr. Lynn is her supervisor.

A Dawn, welcome to the company.

B Thank you, Mr. Lynn.

A The first thing you should know is that you always need to wear your coveralls and gloves when you go into the assembly room.

B I've got them right here.

Now use the dialog to talk about what to wear at your jobs.

SURVEY

Special clothing and equipment can be worn for many reasons. Ask your classmates about their work clothes and equipment. Make a list showing their jobs and the clothing they wear. Then write the reasons for what they wear.

Talk About It

Clocking In and Clocking Out

1. Punch time cards at the beginning and end of each shift.

2. Punch time cards when leaving and returning from lunch or dinner.

3. DO NOT punch time cards for 15-minute breaks.

4. Sign time cards every Friday.

5. Speak to your supervisor to make changes in time cards.

 PRACTICE THE DIALOG

A Excuse me, Ms. Bullock?

B Yes, Ricardo?

A Do I have to punch out at lunch time?

B Yes, you punch out and back in for lunch.

A What about when we take breaks?

B No, you don't have to punch out or in for breaks.

A Thank you, Ms. Bullock.

Useful Language

Please.

Pardon me.

Mr./Miss/Ms./Mrs.

Certainly/Of course.

clock in/clock out

 PARTNER WORK

Take turns talking about rules at work. Ask your partner questions.
Use polite language and correct titles. Use the dialog, the picture,
and the Useful Language above.

ASAP
PROJECT

Your class is writing an employee handbook. Team 1 writes rules for dressing
at work. Team 2 writes rules for breaks, sick days, and vacations. Team 3 writes
about other kinds of rules at work. Share information. Make suggestions for
changes, and write a final version for the employee handbook. Complete this
project as you work through this unit.

Keep Talking

Following company rules

PARTNER WORK

What are they doing wrong? What should they do to be better workers?

NO FOOD OR DRINKS

PRACTICE THE DIALOG

Stella is sick today. Mr. Wu is her supervisor.

A Hello, Mr. Wu? This is Stella. I have the flu. I can't come to work today.

B Thanks for calling me. Get some rest and call me if you're still sick tomorrow.

A All right, Mr. Wu. Thanks.

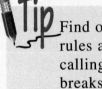

Tip Find out your company's rules about arriving late, calling in sick, taking breaks, and dressing correctly.

PARTNER WORK

Practice calling in sick. Be sure to explain what's the matter. Use the dialog above.

Personal Dictionary ▶ Getting Along at Work

Write the words and phrases that you need to know.

_____

_____

Unit 6

Listening  Understanding company rules
....

 LISTEN AND CIRCLE

What are the rules about? Circle your answer.

1. clothing (sick days) arriving late clocking in

2. clothing sick days arriving late clocking in

3. clothing sick days arriving late clocking in

4. clothing sick days arriving late clocking in

 LISTEN AGAIN

Which rule goes with each company? Write the letter.

—— *c* —— 1. Green Technologies

—————— 2. Rosetti Macaroni

—————— 3. Garden Restaurant

—————— 4. King's Department Store

a. Call if you are going to be late.

b. Punch in every morning and punch out every night.

c. You can take nine sick days a year.

d. You have to wear black shoes.

 LISTEN ONCE MORE

Answer the questions.

1. Who do employees at Green Technologies call when they're sick?

   They call their supervisor.

2. What do you do if you forget to punch in or punch out at Rosetti Macaroni?

   _____

3. What do the waiters and waitresses at the Garden Restaurant wear to work?

   _____

4. What happens at King's Department Store if an employee arrives late three times?

   _____

Unit 6

Grammar
Learning the language you need

A. Study the Examples

Please take	this	memo to customer service.
	that	

Please fill	these	boxes.
	those	

> **Tip** Use *this* and *these* for objects that are close by. Use *that* and *those* for objects that are farther away.

COMPLETE THE SENTENCES

Circle *this*, *that*, *these*, or *those*.

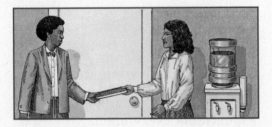

Patricia, can you please take _____

(**this,** **that**) report to Mr. Alvarez?

Ms. Soto, _____ (**this, that**) flower order needs to go out today, please.

Hey, Alex, can you help me move

_____ (**these, those**) boxes?

Can you put _____ (**these, those**) magazines on the shelves?

B. Study the Examples

What time	do	I	stop?
		we	
		you	
		they	
	does	he	
		she	
		it	

I	stop	at 3:15.
We		
You		
They		
He	stops	
She		
It		

Unit 6

A What time _____does_____ the plant _____close_____ (**close**)?

B It _____ (**close**) at 8:00.

A What time _____ Al _____ (**come**) in to work?

B I think he _____ (**come**) in at 1:00.

A What time _____ you _____ (**leave**) today?

B I _____ (**leave**) at 5:30.

C. Study the Examples

Do	I	speak to the manager?
	we	
	you	
	they	
Does	he	
	she	

Yes,	I	do.
	she	does.

No,	I	don't.
	he	doesn't.

COMPLETE THE SENTENCES

Write *do* or *does* and *don't* or *doesn't*.

1. _____Do_____ they work on weekends?

2. No, they _____ .

3. _____ he get to work on time?

4. Yes, he _____ .

PARTNER WORK

Ask your partner questions about work schedules, breaks at work, and dress policies. Follow the dialog below.

A Do you take a break in the afternoon?

B Yes, I do. I take a break after 2:00 every day. How about you?

TEAM WORK

Play Twenty Questions. Think of a job. Do not say the name of the job. Other team members ask you questions about the job. They cannot ask more than 20 questions. You answer *yes* or *no*. The team tries to figure out the job.

READ MARTA'S JOB EVALUATION

EMPLOYEE EVALUATION

Name: **Marta Obregon** Title: **Data Entry Clerk** Date: **4/5/99**

Circle the number. 5 is the highest rating. 1 is the lowest.

1. The employee is punctual. She/He arrives on time and ready for work.

1	②	3	4	5
poor		satisfactory		excellent

Comments: **Marta sometimes arrives late. She is working to improve this problem.**

2. The employee is always dressed correctly.

1	2	3	4	⑤
poor		satisfactory		excellent

Comments: **Marta is always neat and professional. She is an example to others.**

3. The employee is polite and pleasant to superiors and other employees.

1	2	3	④	5
poor		satisfactory		excellent

Comments: **Marta is always polite, with a smile or a friendly word for her coworkers.**

4. The employee is flexible and willing to do different things if the supervisor or a coworker asks.

1	2	3	④	5
poor		satisfactory		excellent

Comments: **Marta is always willing to help her coworkers.**

ANSWER THE QUESTIONS

1. What is Marta's job? _____ *She's a data entry clerk.* _____

2. What does Marta need to improve? _____

3. Does Marta dress well for her job? _____

4. What does Marta do for her coworkers? _____

DISCUSSION

Do you think Marta is a good employee? How can Marta change to improve her work? Do you know someone who needs to improve his or her work?

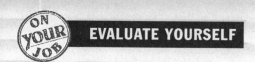

EMPLOYEE EVALUATION

Name: _____ **Title:** _____ **Date:** _____

Circle the number. 5 is the highest rating. 1 is the lowest.

1. The employee is punctual. She/He arrives on time and ready for work.

1	2	3	4	5
poor		satisfactory		excellent

Comments: _____

2. The employee is always dressed correctly.

1	2	3	4	5
poor		satisfactory		excellent

Comments: _____

3. The employee is polite and pleasant to superiors and other employees.

1	2	3	4	5
poor		satisfactory		excellent

Comments: _____

4. The employee is flexible and willing to do different things if the supervisor or a coworker asks.

1	2	3	4	5
poor		satisfactory		excellent

Comments: _____

 PARTNER WORK

Read your evaluation. Think about what it says. What would you like to improve? How can you improve your work? Talk about your ideas with your partner.

DISCUSSION

Talk about the kind of people you like to work with. What are the traits of a good employee and coworker? What can you do when you work with someone who is difficult?

Unit 6

READ THE ARTICLE

Read this article from the *Newton News*.

NEWTON NEWS
page 12

Politeness on the Job

At work, do you ever hear people saying things like this:
"What do you want?"
"Go away. I'm busy."
"Move. You're in my way."

No one said *please*, *thank you*, or *excuse me*. These words are important on the job. They can make the workplace a pleasant place. Being polite

is a simple thing to do, but it makes a big difference.
Listen to what people say at your workplace. Do you hear polite words?

ANSWER THE QUESTIONS

Are the people being polite? Write *yes* or *no*.

A "Give me that hammer right now."   *no*

B "I'm busy. I'll give it to you later."   _____

A "You're blocking the door. I need to get through."   _____

B "Oh, excuse me."   _____

PARTNER WORK

Which parts of the dialog above are not polite?
Take turns saying them with polite language.

 *Culture Notes*

In North America, people often say, "Hi, how are you?" Are they being polite? Are they really asking for information about you? What do you answer to be polite?

Performance Check

Complete the activities. Go over your work with a partner or your teacher. Then complete the Performance Review on page 74.

SKILL 1　FOLLOW COMPANY RULES

Do they follow the rules for work? What should they do? Tell your partner or teacher what each employee should do.

Dress Code for Circle Department Store: Clean shirt and pants. Name tag. No sneakers.

Late Policy for Block Technology: Any employee who arrives late must report to the supervisor immediately.

SKILL 2　CALL IN SICK

Call in sick. Your teacher or partner is your boss.

SKILL 3　USE POLITE LANGUAGE

Are the dialogs polite? How can you change what they say to be more polite? Tell a partner or your teacher.

1. **A** Hey, Marcos, help me. I want to leave early tonight.

   B All right, all right. Just wait a minute.

   A Come on, Marcos. I want to go now.

2. **A** Put these boxes on the shelves right away.

   B I can't help you right now. I'm doing something else.

   A This is more important.

Unit 6

Rate yourself as an employee. If you choose *needs improvement*, say why. How can you change your work habits to meet your company's expectations?

Employee Self Evaluation

Name: _____

Circle the word that best describes your work.

1. Punctuality. Do you arrive at work on time?

good　　　　　average　　　　　needs improvement

2. Dress. Is your clothing or uniform neat and complete?

good　　　　　average　　　　　needs improvement

3. Politeness. Are you courteous and polite to other employees and customers?

good　　　　　average　　　　　needs improvement

4. Helpfulness. Are you willing to help your coworkers?

good　　　　　average　　　　　needs improvement

Performance Review

I can...

☐ **1.** follow company rules.

☐ **2.** call in sick.

☐ **3.** use polite language.

☐ **4.** improve my performance.

DISCUSSION

Work with a team. How will the skills help you? Make a list. Share the list with your class.

What do you think?

Look at the pictures.

What are the people doing?

Do you handle money at work?

Do you take your paycheck to the bank?

Performance Preview

Can you...

☐ 1. count money?

☐ 2. fill out a time card?

☐ 3. make a deposit?

☐ 4. understand a W-4 form?

PARTNER WORK

Talk about the coins and bills on the desk. How much is each one worth?
How do you say the names of coins and bills?

penny	nickel	dime	quarter	one dollar bill
five dollar bill		ten dollar bill		twenty dollar bill

TEAM WORK

Look at the dollar amounts. Say how many of each bill and coin you need.
Make two or three different combinations of bills and coins for each amount.

1. $1.25   **2.** $15.75   **3.** $42.50   **4.** $9.64   **5.** $4.37   **6.** $27.93

SURVEY

Do you get paid in cash or by check at
work? Do you have your pay deposited
directly into your account? Ask your
classmates. Make a bar graph. Label the
first bar *cash*. Label the second bar *check*.
Label the third bar *direct deposit*.
Follow the example.

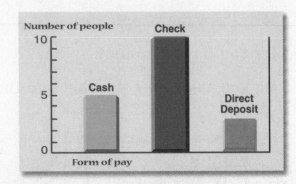

Bay State Telephone Company

Day	Start Time	Lunch out	Lunch in	Finish Time	Total Hours
Monday	7:30	11:30	12:30	4:30	8
Tuesday	8:00	12:30	1:30	5:00	8
Wednesday	7:45	12:00	1:00	4:45	8
Thursday	7:30	11:00	12:00	4:30	8
Friday	—	—	—	—	0

Total Hours __32__ Hourly Rate __$7.00__ Total Pay __$224.00__

Employee Signature __Maria Hernandez__ Date __12/10/99__

PRACTICE THE DIALOG

A Luis, can you help me with my time card?

B Sure. Let's take a look. How many hours did you work last week?

A 32 hours.

B You make $7.00 an hour. For 32 hours your total should be $224.00. That's what you filled in. It looks fine.

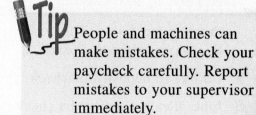

Tip People and machines can make mistakes. Check your paycheck carefully. Report mistakes to your supervisor immediately.

PARTNER WORK

Look at the pay rates and the number of hours. Figure out each person's pay. Then talk about the information. Use the dialog above.

1. 33 hours at $9 per hour   **2.** 39 hours at $7 per hour   **3.** 24 hours at $5 per hour

ASAP
PROJECT

As a class, create a chart of services for two local banks. Divide into two teams. Each team finds out a bank's name, address, telephone number, hours of operation, types of accounts, interest rates, fees, minimum balances, service charges, and other services. Complete this project as you work through this unit.

Keep Talking — Using the bank

PARTNER WORK

Complete the bank deposit slip. Sign the back of the check.

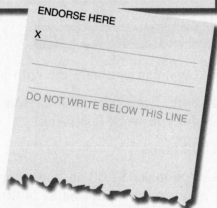

DEPOSIT SLIP

LAURA MORTON
45 LARK CIRCLE
MELROSE, MI 98761

DATE _____

Deposits may not be available for immediate withdrawal.

_____
Sign here for cash received (if required).

Thrifty Bank

CASH			
CHECKS 1235	6 3 4	1	2
SUB-TOTAL	6 3 4	1	2
LESS CASH RECEIVED			
$		.	

ENDORSE HERE

X _____

DO NOT WRITE BELOW THIS LINE

PRACTICE THE DIALOG

Practice the dialog. Then use the dialog to cash and deposit checks.

A I'd like to deposit this check.

B Fine. Please endorse the check.

A Do I sign here?

B That's correct. Here's your receipt.

A Thanks.

Personal Dictionary ▶ Finances

Write the words and phrases that you need to know.

_____

_____

_____

 LISTEN AND CIRCLE

Listen and circle the money amount you hear.

1. $1.25   ($12.25) $12.50

2. $7.99 $8.99 $9.99

3. $102.65 $112.65 $122.65

4. $.05 $.50 $5.00

 LISTEN AGAIN

Write *cash* or *check.*

1. <u>cash</u>   2. _____

3. _____   4. _____

> **Tip** There are many ways to say different amounts of money. For example, here are four ways to say $1.25.
>
> **one dollar and twenty-five cents**
> **a dollar twenty-five**
> **one twenty-five**
> **a dollar and a quarter**

 LISTEN AND WRITE

Listen and fill in the check.

The Frame Shop   1203
1500 Alameda Boulevard
Austin, TX 78731

PAY TO THE
ORDER OF _____ $ | 329.47 |

_____ DOLLARS

LANDMARK BANK
124 Shady Lane
Austin, Texas 79079

SAMPLE

FOR _____ _____

Grammar

Learning the language you need

A. Study the Examples

| How many | checks | are there? |

| There's | a check. |
| There are | checks. |

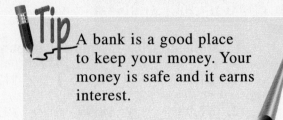

Tip A bank is a good place to keep your money. Your money is safe and it earns interest.

COMPLETE THE DIALOG

Pedro is a warehouse manager. He and Betty are taking inventory.

A How many boxes of the $1.50 rubber tubing _____are there_____ ?

B Let's see. _____ only one box left.

A How about copper wire? How many rolls _____ ?

B _____ four of the $30 rolls.

A How many cases of liquid cleaner _____ ?

B _____ one case back here.

B. Study the Examples

| Is | there | a W-4 tax form? |
| Are | | tax forms? |

| Yes, | there | is. |
| | | are. |

| No, | there | isn't. |
| | | aren't. |

COMPLETE THE DIALOG

Lana has a new job. She has some questions for the office manager.

A _____Is there_____ a place to sign in every day?

B Yes, _____ . It's just inside the entrance.

A _____ any forms I need to fill out?

B Yes, _____ a few tax and payroll forms.

A _____ any other things I need to know?

B No, _____ . See you on Monday.

C. Study the Examples

Which	line do I sign my name on?
	space is for checks?

Look at the check register. Write questions using *which*.

Check Number	Date	Description	Amount of Payment (−)		Amount of Deposit (+)		Balance	
							1465	93
767	5/9	Warehouse Office Supply	102	35			1363	58
768	5/11	Change Computer Systems	250	00			1113	58
	5/13	Deposit			310	00	1423	58
769	5/17	Parkway Truck Repair	69	89			1353	69
770	5/18	Helpful Temporaries	391	00			962	69

1. _____ Which check is for Helpful Temporaries? _____

Check number 770 is for Helpful Temporaries.

2. _____

Check number 769 is for $69.89.

PARTNER WORK

Look at the check register again. Take turns asking questions using *which*.
For example, "Which check is the largest?" Then fill out the deposit slip for
the deposit.

DEPOSIT SLIP

CASH

DATE_____

Deposits may not be available for immediate withdrawal.

C H E C K S

310 00

Sign here for cash received (if required).

CENTURY SAVINGS BANK

Arlington, VA

SUB-TOTAL

LESS CASH RECEIVED

$

Reading and Writing

LOOK AT THE TIME CARD

SPOTLESS CLEANERS

PO BOX 9881 NEWTON, MA 02164

9/17/99
WEEK ENDING DATE

000-58-4343
SOCIAL SECURITY NUMBER

Maria Valdez
EMPLOYEE SIGNATURE

John Cho
SUPERVISOR SIGNATURE

OFFICE CODE
(Office use only)

PRINT FIRMLY

	START TIME	LUNCH OUT / IN		FINISH TIME	DAILY HOURS WORKED
SU					
MO	10:00	12:30	1:30	7:00	8
TU	8:00	11:30	12:30	5:00	8
WE	7:30	11:00	11:30	2:00	6
TH	8:00	12:00	12:30	4:00	7½
FR	9:30	1:30	2:30	6:30	8
SA					
TOTAL HOURS FOR WEEK					**37½**

ANSWER THE QUESTIONS

1. Who has to sign the time card?

   the employee and the supervisor

2. When does Maria take her lunch on Tuesday?

   _____

3. Which day does Maria work for only six hours?

   _____

4. What week is the time card for?

   _____

DISCUSSION

What other information can you find on Maria's time card? Is it easy to read and understand? Why or why not? Why do you think it says *print firmly*? Does your time card ask for similar information?

Unit 7

You work part time at Spotless Cleaners. Fill out the time card for the hours you worked this week. Be sure to follow the instructions and fill out the time card completely.

PRINT FIRMLY

SPOTLESS CLEANERS

PO BOX 9881 NEWTON, MA 02164

	START TIME	LUNCH OUT / IN	FINISH TIME	DAILY HOURS WORKED
SU				
MO				
TU				
WE				
TH				
FR				
SA				

WEEK ENDING DATE
_____

SOCIAL SECURITY NUMBER
_____

EMPLOYEE SIGNATURE
_____

SUPERVISOR SIGNATURE

OFFICE CODE
(Office use only)

TOTAL HOURS FOR WEEK

WRITE THE AMOUNT

Look at your time card. You make $9.00 per hour.

How much should your paycheck be? _____

DISCUSSION

Time cards and other forms use a lot of abbreviations. Abbreviations are short forms of words. For example, on this time card *SU* stands for Sunday. Look at the time card. What are some other abbreviations? What do they stand for? Make a list.

READ THE W-4 FORM

A W-4 form is a government tax form. The W-4 form tells your employer how much money to take out of your paycheck for federal taxes.

Form **W-4**	**Employee's Withholding Allowance Certificate**	OMB No. 1545-0010
Department of the Treasury Internal Revenue Service	► **For Privacy Act and Paperwork Reduction Act Notice, see reverse.**	

1 Type or print your first name and middle initial	Last name	**2** Your social security number
Emil L.	Sobodka	000 : 45 : 6789

Home address (number and street or rural route)	**3** ☐ Single ☒ Married ☐ Married, but withhold at higher Single rate.
1856 N. Kostner Ave.	Note: *If married, but legally separated, or spouse is a nonresident alien, check the Single box.*

City or town, state, and ZIP code	**4** If your last name differs from that on your social security card, check
Chicago, IL 60608	here and call 1-800-772-1213 for a new card . . . . . ► ☐

5 Total number of allowances you are claiming (from line G above or from the worksheets on page 2 if they apply) . | **5** | 6

6 Additional amount, if any, you want withheld from each paycheck . . . . | **6** | $

7 I claim exemption from withholding for **(year)** and I certify that I meet **BOTH** of the following conditions for exemption:
● Last year I had a right to a refund of **ALL** Federal income tax withheld because I had **NO** tax liability; **AND**
● This year I expect a refund of **ALL** Federal income tax withheld because I expect to have **NO** tax liability.
If you meet both conditions, enter "EXEMPT" here . . . . ► | **7**

Under penalties of perjury, I certify that I am entitled to the number of withholding allowances claimed on this certificate or entitled to claim exempt status.

Employee's signature ► *Emil L. Sobodka*   **Date** ► *February 23, 1999*

8 Employer's name and address (Employer: Complete 8 and 10 only if sending to the IRS)	**9** Office code (optional)	**10** Employer identification number

CIRCLE

What information does a W-4 form ask for?
Circle the numbers.

1. your address

2. your Social Security number

3. the names of your children

4. the date

5. your date of birth

6. whether you are single or married

 Tip If you change your name when you get married, get a new Social Security card with your new name. This will make filing your tax forms much easier.

 **Culture Notes**

How do you fill out your tax forms? Do you fill them out yourself? Do you get help from an accountant or tax preparer? Why or why not? If you need help, who do you ask? Do you call the IRS or visit an IRS office?

Performance Check

Complete the activities. Go over your work with a partner or your teacher. Then complete the Performance Review on Page 86.

SKILL 1	COUNT MONEY

Write the amount of money.

1.

2.

3.

_____   _____   _____

SKILL 2	FILL OUT A TIME CARD

Complete the time card.

- You worked 8 hours on Monday.

- You worked 9 hours on Tuesday.

- You took a day off on Wednesday.

- You worked 8 hours on Thursday.

- You worked 9 hours on Friday.

- You worked 6 hours on Saturday.

XYZ Company
Employee Time Card

Name _____

Week ending _____

Day	Hours worked
	Total Hours

Supervisor
Signature _____

Your pay check is for $327.19. Deposit it. Fill out the deposit slip and endorse your check.

DEPOSIT SLIP

CASH

CHECKS

DATE _____
Deposits may not be available for immediate withdrawal.

_____
Sign here for cash received (if required).

SUB-TOTAL

LESS CASH
RECEIVED

Thrifty Bank

$ | . |

ENDORSE HERE

X _____

_____

DO NOT WRITE BELOW THIS LINE

SKILL 4 **UNDERSTAND A W-4 FORM**

Write *yes* or *no*.

1. A W-4 form is a government tax form. _____

2. You need to know your Social Security _____
number to fill out a W-4 form.

3. You need to put your children's names _____
on a W-4 form.

Performance Review

I can...

☐ 1. count money.
☐ 2. fill out a time card.
☐ 3. make a deposit.
☐ 4. understand a W-4 form.

DISCUSSION

Work with a team. How will these skills help you? Make a list.
Share your list with the class.

Health and Safety

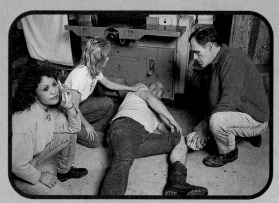

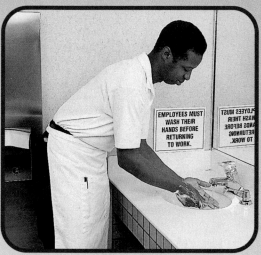

What do you think?

Look at the pictures.

What are the people doing?

Are they wearing safety equipment?

Are there safety rules where you work?

What are they?

Performance Preview

Can you...

☐ 1. identify parts of the body?

☐ 2. handle an emergency?

☐ 3. describe an injury or illness?

☐ 4. read safety signs?

☐ 5. follow safety instructions?

TEAM WORK

Identify as many parts of the body as you can. Write the words on the lines.

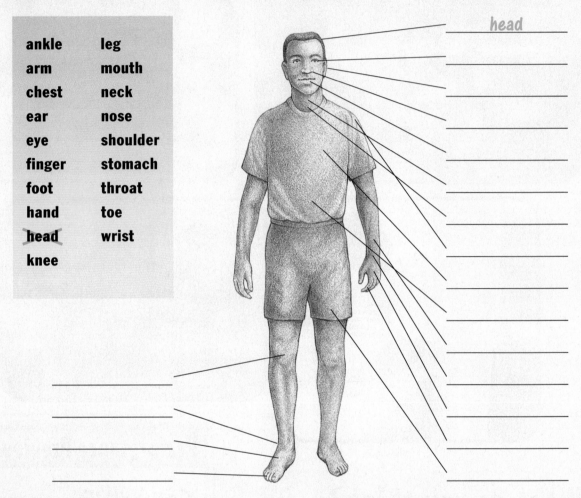

ankle	leg
arm	mouth
chest	neck
ear	nose
eye	shoulder
finger	stomach
foot	throat
hand	toe
~~head~~	wrist
knee	

head

PARTNER WORK

Student A points to a part of the body.
Student B names it.

A What's this?

B That's his foot.

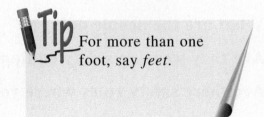

Tip For more than one foot, say *feet*.

SURVEY

How many students have had a broken arm? A broken leg? Make 2 lists.

Talk About It

Calling 911

PRACTICE THE DIALOG

A This is the 911 operator. May I have your name and phone number?

B Marta Roca. 555-9021.

A What's the emergency, Marta?

B There's a fire in the back of the building!

A What's the address?

B 765 Long Street. It's the Roca Laundry Service.

A That's 765 Long Street. I'm sending the fire department right away.

B Please hurry!

Useful Language

immediately/right away

There's a fire/an accident/ an injury.

Please send an ambulance/ the police/a fire truck.

PARTNER WORK

Look at the pictures. Take turns being the caller or the 911 operator. Call about these emergencies. Use the dialog and the Useful Language above.

ASAP PROJECT

As a class, create a set of emergency procedures for your workplace or school. Include procedures for fires and bad weather. Make a list of emergency telephone numbers. Complete this project as you work through this unit.

Keep Talking

PARTNER WORK

What's wrong? Look at the pictures. Say what you think is wrong with each person.

  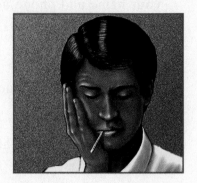

 PRACTICE THE DIALOG

Galena is injured at work. She describes the injury to the company nurse.

A What's the matter?

B I cut my finger.

A Does it hurt?

B Not too much, but it's bleeding.

A Well, it doesn't look too serious. I'll put a bandage on it.

B Thanks.

Useful Language

What's wrong?

I have a broken arm/wrist/leg.

I hurt my back.

I have a fever/temperature/burn.

I have a headache/stomachache/toothache.

I feel sick.

It hurts.

PARTNER WORK

You are one of the people in the pictures. Tell your partner what's wrong and how you were injured or became ill. Use the dialog and the Useful Language above.

 Personal Dictionary ▶ Health and Safety

Write the words and phrases that you need to know.

_____

_____

_____

Listening

Following safety instructions

LISTEN AND NUMBER

Listen to the instructions. Number the instructions in order.

__3__ Close the door behind you.   _____ Walk to the nearest exit.

_____ Turn off all of the lights.   _____ Go down the stairs.

_____ Walk to the northwest corner.

LISTEN AND CIRCLE

Listen to the emergencies. Who should you call? Circle the symbol.

1.

2.

3.

LISTEN AND WRITE

| Call | Call | Cover | Find | Stay | Stay | Tell | Wait |

Listen to the emergency calls. What do you need to do?

1. _____Cover_____ him with a blanket. _____ for an ambulance.

2. _____ everyone to leave the building. _____ outside the building.

3. _____ the container. _____ the poison control center.

4. _____ a tow truck. _____ in the van.

Unit 8

Grammar

Learning the language you need
....

A. Study the Examples

How	do	I	feel?
		we	
		you	
		they	
	does	he	
		she	
		it	

I	feel	fine.
We		
You		
They		
He	feels	
She		
It		

HOW DO THEY FEEL?

Write how you think they feel.

sick	happy	tired	sad

She feels happy.
_____   _____   _____

PARTNER WORK

Read each situation. How do you feel? What do you do? Talk with your partner.

1. Your boss thanks you for your hard work.

2. You have a stomachache.

3. You are late to work in the morning.

4. You see an accident at work.

5. You are employee of the month.

afraid	nervous
angry	sick
happy	terrible

92

Unit 8

B. Study the Examples

I	have	the flu.
We		
You		
They		
She	has	
He		

✏️ **Tip** Most buildings have emergency exits and fire extinguishers. Locate these at your workplace or school.

COMPLETE THE SENTENCES

Look at the pictures. Complete the sentences.

1. __They have__ the flu.

2. _____ a broken arm.

3. _____ a burn.

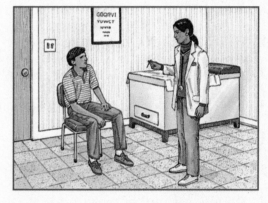

4. _____ a fever.

TEAM WORK

What do you do when you or someone in your family is sick?
What do you do when you are sick or injured at work or school?

Unit 8

93

Reading and Writing

READ THE SAFETY AND WARNING SIGNS

1. **EXIT**

2. **CAUTION WET FLOOR**

3. **DANGER HARD HAT —AREA—**

4. **High Voltage KEEP OUT**

5. **FIRE ALARM**

6. **NOTICE No food or drinks in this area**

7. **WATCH YOUR STEP**

8. **SAFETY GLASSES AND GLOVES REQUIRED**

PARTNER WORK

Answer the questions. Write the numbers. Talk about what each sign means.

1. Which sign tells you where to leave a building? _____ 1

2. Which signs tell you to wear special clothing? _____

3. Which sign do you look for when there's a fire? _____

4. Which sign tells people not to eat or drink? _____

5. Which signs tell you to be careful? _____

6. Do you see any of these signs at work? Which ones? _____

ON YOUR JOB DISCUSSION

What safety or warning signs can you see in these places?

a restaurant   a construction site   a subway station

a chemical laboratory   a school   an office building

Write what's wrong? What happens?

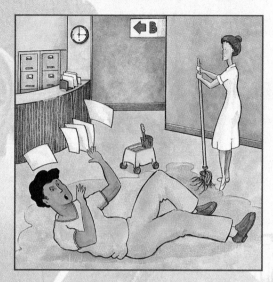

The floor is wet.

He falls down.

DISCUSSION

What kind of accidents do you think happen most often at work?
What can you do to prevent these kinds of accidents or injuries?

Extension

Reading safety instructions

READ THE FIRE SAFETY PROCEDURES

IN CASE OF FIRE

1. Pull the nearest fire alarm.
2. Use the map to find the nearest exit.
3. Exit the building quickly, but DO NOT run.
4. DO NOT use the elevators. Use the stairs.
5. Cross the street in front of the building. Meet with your supervisor.
6. DO NOT go back into the building for any reason.
7. Follow all the instructions given by your supervisor and the fire department.

ANSWER THE QUESTIONS

1. What do you do first if there is a fire? _____ *pull the fire alarm* _____

2. Can you return to the building to get your tools? _____

3. Do you use the elevator or the stairs during a fire? _____

4. Where do you meet your supervisor? _____

PARTNER WORK

What other kinds of emergencies can there be? Talk about safety procedures you would follow in these situations:

1. There is a tornado or other weather emergency.

2. The electricity has gone out all over the building.

ON YOUR JOB *Culture Notes*

Do the employees where you work know first aid or CPR? Where can you get this kind of training? Do you think it is important for people to have these skills? Why?

Complete the activities. Go over your work with a partner or your teacher. Then complete the Performance Review on Page 98.

SKILL 1   IDENTIFY PARTS OF THE BODY

Write the names of the parts of the body.

arm	mouth
chest	neck
ear	nose
eye	shoulder
finger	stomach
hand	throat
head	wrist

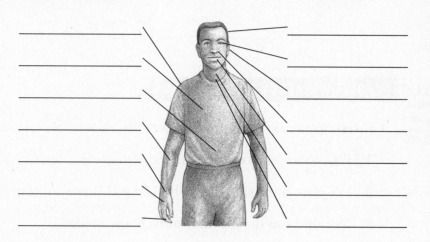

SKILL 2   HANDLE AN EMERGENCY

Work with a partner. Call 911 to report one of these emergencies.

1. You pass a car accident on your way to work.

2. There is a fire in the kitchen where you work.

3. One of your coworkers got gasoline on her face.

SKILL 3   DESCRIBE AN INJURY OR ILLNESS

What's wrong with the people? Tell your partner or your teacher.

Unit 8

Are they following the signs? Write *yes* or *no*.

_____   _____   _____

SKILL 5 | **FOLLOW SAFETY INSTRUCTIONS**

Listen to the instructions. Answer the questions. Circle *yes* or *no*.

1. Will there be a warning signal if there's a tornado?   yes   no

2. Do you go outside of the building if there's a tornado?   yes   no

3. Can you use the elevator during a tornado?   yes   no

Performance Review

I can...

- ☐ **1.** identify parts of the body.
- ☐ **2.** handle an emergency.
- ☐ **3.** describe an injury or illness.
- ☐ **4.** read safety signs.
- ☐ **5.** follow safety instructions.

DISCUSSION

Work with a team. How will these skills help you? Make a list.
Share your list with the class.

What do you think?

Look at the pictures.

What are the people doing?

Do you usually work alone or with others?

Do you show someone else how to do a job?

Performance Preview

Can you...

- [ ] 1. give and receive feedback?
- [ ] 2. talk about job duties?
- [ ] 3. evaluate your work?
- [ ] 4. identify job skills?

Getting Started

Look at the pictures. Write the letter of the person next to his or her job duties. Then make a list of other job duties the people in the pictures might have. Share your list with the class.

a. receptionist   **b.** security guard   **3.** bellhop

_b_____ check all the doors, halls, and stairs

_____ show guests to their rooms

_____ greet visitors

_____ carry luggage to guests' rooms

_____ answer the telephone

_____ check the alarms

PARTNER WORK

Student A asks about someone in the pictures. Student B answers.

A Who answers the telephone?

B A receptionist.

SURVEY

What are your duties at work or at home? Make a list. Then, as a class, make a list of everyone's duties. Look at the list. Which job duties are most common?

PRACTICE THE DIALOG

A Hi, Victor. You're doing very well your first week.

B Thanks, Dave. I still have a lot to learn.

A One of your job duties is to turn off the lights at closing time.
You left some of the lights on last night.

B I'm sorry.

A Don't worry about it. I'll show you tonight.

B Thanks for the help.

A Sure. Let's get started.

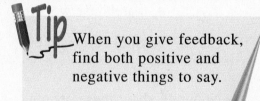

Tip When you give feedback, find both positive and negative things to say.

PARTNER WORK

You're in charge of the dishwashers at Fabulous Food Service. Your partner is a new employee. Today your partner forgot to put soap in the dishwashing machine. Talk to your partner. Use the dialog above.

ASAP
PROJECT

You and your classmates work at Grand Supermarket. Choose a job at the supermarket (such as cashier, stocker, bagger). Make a chart. Team 1 writes the job duties. Team 2 writes the skills someone needs for the job. Team 3 writes the steps for training someone to do the job. Complete this project as you work through this unit.

Unit 9

Keep Talking

 PRACTICE THE DIALOG

A and B are looking for an employee to work on a new project.

A We're getting some new machines. Who's a good mechanic?

B Jean. She's really good at fixing machines.

A Great. Let's meet with Jean.

Useful Language

We're getting very busy.

We need another data entry clerk.

We need a new child care worker.

PARTNER WORK

Match the jobs to the people. Write the letter.

_____b____ **1.** medical technician

_____ **2.** auto mechanic

_____ **3.** data entry clerk

_____ **4.** warehouse worker

_____ **5.** child care worker

a. Li enjoys working with children.

b. Marta can use X-ray equipment.

c. Ed can drive a forklift.

d. Marcos can work with tools and fix engines.

e. Sabrina knows how to use computers.

Now talk about these people and their jobs. Use the dialog and the Useful Language above.

Personal Dictionary ▶ Job Skills and Duties

Write the words and phrases that you need to know.

_____

_____

_____

LISTEN AND WRITE

Listen to the dialogs. Who can do the job? Write the letter of the picture.

1. ___a___   **2.** _____   **3.** _____

LISTEN AND CIRCLE

Circle the letter of the statement that describes each employee's performance.

1. a. Cindy gets to work on time every day.

   b. Cindy is sometimes late to work.

2. a. Enrique is usually polite to customers on the phone.

   b. Enrique is not polite to customers on the phone.

3. a. Hans is not a good driver.

   b. Hans drives safely.

4. a. Maria always enjoys working with other employees.

   b. Maria doesn't always enjoy working with other employees.

Discussion

Imagine that you're giving the employees in the dialogs feedback. What do you say? How can each person do a better job? Listen to the dialogs again if you need help.

A. Study the Examples

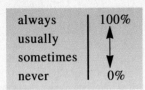

> I always arrive at work on time.
> I'm never late.

COMPLETE THE SENTENCES

Write about yourself and how you do your job. Use *always*, *usually*, *sometimes*, and *never*.

1. I _____

2. I _____ .

3. I _____ .

4. I _____ .

PARTNER WORK

Ask questions about how often your partner does things at work. Follow the dialog below. Use these words and some of your own.

start	finish	ask	answer	teach	learn

A Do you usually get to work on time?

B Yes, I'm usually on time.

B. Study the Examples

> I always keep my work area clean.

> I'm cleaning my work area now.

Unit 9

COMPLETE THE SENTENCES

Use the language in B.

1. I usually _____take_____ (**take**) the bus to work.

2. Right now I _____ (**wait**) for the bus.

3. Sometimes my sister _____ (**drive**) me to work.

4. I never _____ (**walk**) to work.

5. I always _____ (**arrive**) at work on time.

WRITE SENTENCES

Use the pairs of words to write your own sentences. Follow the language in B.

1. usually/work ___I usually work on Saturdays.___

2. work/now _____

3. always/take _____

4. take/now _____

5. sometimes/arrive _____

6. arrive/now _____

PARTNER WORK

Imagine you're at work. Talk about what you usually do and what you're doing now.

READ THE EMPLOYEE TRAINING MANUAL

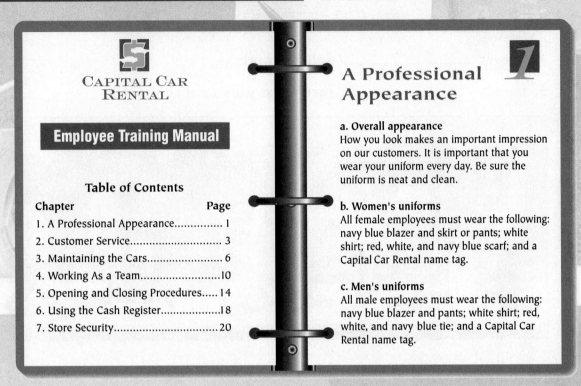

CAPITAL CAR RENTAL

Employee Training Manual

Table of Contents

A Professional Appearance

a. Overall appearance
How you look makes an important impression on our customers. It is important that you wear your uniform every day. Be sure the uniform is neat and clean.

b. Women's uniforms
All female employees must wear the following: navy blue blazer and skirt or pants; white shirt; red, white, and navy blue scarf; and a Capital Car Rental name tag.

c. Men's uniforms
All male employees must wear the following: navy blue blazer and pants; white shirt; red, white, and navy blue tie; and a Capital Car Rental name tag.

Which chapter in the manual tells the employee how to do each task? Write the number.

___3___ **a.** clean the cars

_____ **b.** lock the store at night

_____ **c.** dress appropriately

_____ **d.** greet customers

_____ **e.** work as a team

DISCUSSION

How do training manuals help employees and companies? Does your company have a training manual? Did you learn your job from the manual? Or, did someone show you how to do your job?

Capital Car Rental uses this checklist.

CAPITAL CAR RENTAL

Personal Appearance Checklist

Name _____ Date _____

Overall Appearance

☑ 1. Uniform is neat and clean.

☐ 2. Uniform is complete.

Uniform

☐ 3. Navy blue blazer

☐ 4. Navy blue skirt/pants

☐ 5. White shirt

☐ 6. Red, white, and navy blue scarf/tie

☐ 7. Capital Car Rental name tag

COMPLETE THE CHECKLIST

Capital Car Rental employees work in pairs each day to check their appearance. Each employee completes the checklist for a partner. Look at the picture of Michael. Fill out the checklist for his appearance.

Tip
On any job, find out the rules for what to wear. Some jobs require uniforms. Other jobs have rules about the kinds of clothes you can wear to work. A neat appearance always gives a good impression.

Unit 9

Extension — Evaluating your work

WRITE A SELF EVALUATION

Your supervisor wants you to evaluate your work. Look at the form.
Fill it out about yourself. Then talk over your evaluation with a partner.
Talk about what is good and what can be improved.

Circle the word that best describes your work in each category.

1. Job Knowledge (Do you know all of the duties and responsibilities of your job?)

Excellent   Good   Fair   Poor   Unsatisfactory

How can you improve your job knowledge?

_____

_____

2. Quantity of Work (Do you complete all of your work on time?)

Excellent   Good   Fair   Poor   Unsatisfactory

How can you improve your quantity of work?

_____

_____

3. Quality of Work (How good is the work you do?)

Excellent   Good   Fair   Poor   Unsatisfactory

How can you improve your quality of work?

_____

_____

ON YOUR JOB — Culture Notes

How well do you do your job? Are there some things you can improve?
What are they? Do you want more training? Can you talk to your supervisor
about ways to improve your work or to get more training?

Performance Check

Complete the activities. Go over your work with a partner or your teacher. Then complete the Performance Review on Page 110.

SKILL 1 **GIVE AND RECEIVE FEEDBACK**

You are in charge of the general office clerks. Your partner is a new clerk who typed some mailing labels. Your partner did a good job typing the labels, but did not sort the labels by their zip codes. Give feedback about the work.

SKILL 2 **TALK ABOUT JOB DUTIES**

Make a list of all of the duties at your job or a job you want to have. Explain your duties to your partner or your teacher. Which duties are the most difficult? Which are the easiest?

SKILL 3 **EVALUATE YOUR WORK**

Circle the word that best describes your work at home, at school, or at your job. Then explain your answers to your partner or teacher.

Circle the word that best describes your performance.

1. You arrive at work on time.

| Never | Sometimes | Usually | Always |

2. You work well with other employees.

| Never | Sometimes | Usually | Always |

3. You try to improve your job performance.

| Never | Sometimes | Usually | Always |

Match the jobs to the skills. Write the letter.

_____ **1.** auto mechanic   **a.** likes taking care of children

_____ **2.** day care worker   **b.** knows how to use an X-ray machine

_____ **3.** medical technician   **c.** can fix car engines

_____ **4.** warehouse worker   **d.** can work on a computer

_____ **5.** data entry clerk   **e.** knows how to operate a forklift

Performance Review

I can...

- [ ] **1.** give and receive feedback.
- [ ] **2.** talk about job duties.
- [ ] **3.** evaluate my work.
- [ ] **4.** identify job skills.

DISCUSSION

Work with a team. How will your new skills help you? Make a list.
Share your list with the class.

What do you think?

Look at the pictures.

What are the people doing?

What jobs do they have?

How do you find jobs?

Performance Preview

Can you...

☐ 1. describe your job skills?

☐ 2. read help-wanted ads?

☐ 3. figure out the best job for you?

☐ 4. complete a job application?

Getting Started

TEAM WORK

Look at the picture. What jobs do the people have? What skills do they have?

delivery driver	construction worker	child care worker
grocery clerk	bus driver	police officer

PARTNER WORK

Student A asks a question about someone in the picture.
Student B says what the person can do.

A What can a child care worker do?

B She can take care of children.

 **SURVEY**

Make a chart that shows everyone's jobs and skills. Write the names of all of the jobs you and your classmates have had. Next to each job write the skills you need for the job.

Unit 10

Talk About It

PRACTICE THE DIALOG

A Hi, Bettina. How's school?

B Great, Claudette. I'm studying air conditioning repair. And you? What are you doing these days?

A I'm looking for a job. I want to be a child care worker.

B That's a good job for you. Good luck.

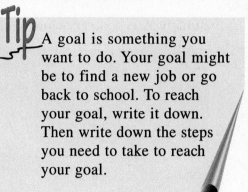

Tip A goal is something you want to do. Your goal might be to find a new job or go back to school. To reach your goal, write it down. Then write down the steps you need to take to reach your goal.

PARTNER WORK

Your partner is one of the people in the pictures. Find out what your partner is doing these days. Take turns. Follow the dialog above.

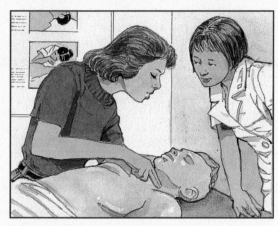

I'm studying first aid.

I'm taking truck-driving classes.

ASAP PROJECT

As a class, write a *Job Hunter's Guide*. Use the information from the Survey. Team 1 writes job titles and skills needed. Team 2 finds the names of possible employers. Team 3 organizes the information and types or writes it neatly for the guide. Complete this project as you work through this unit.

Unit 10

PRACTICE THE DIALOG

Student A is a career counselor. Student B is looking for a job.

A What kind of job are you looking for?

B I'd like to be carpenter.

A What job skills do you have?

B I can measure and cut wood.

A Do you have any experience?

B Yes, I was a carpenter's helper for two years.

PARTNER WORK

Ask and answer questions about jobs you would like to have. Talk about your skills. Use the dialog and the Useful Language above.

Useful Language

drive trucks	gardener
paint houses	medical technician
bake cakes	
use X-ray machines	cook
	painter
prepare meals	baker
cut grass	delivery driver

Personal Dictionary ▸ Getting the Job You Want

Write the words and phrases that you need to know.

 **Listening** ···· **Understanding want ads** ········

 LISTEN AND CIRCLE

Listen and circle the jobs the people are calling about.

1. hairdresser

(truck driver)

auto mechanic

2. nurse's aide

gardener

hairdresser

3. cook

gardener

hairdresser

4. nurse's aide

truck driver

gardener

 LISTEN AGAIN

Read the questions about their training and skills. Circle the answers.

1. Does Kevin have three years of experience?   (yes)   no

2. Does Clara have her hairdresser's license?   yes   no

3. Can Carlos use a lawn mower?   yes   no

4. Does Suzy have a nurse's aide certificate?   yes   no

 LISTEN AND CIRCLE

Pablo Bueno is calling about a job. Read the questions. Circle the answers.

1. What job is Pablo calling about?   (gardener)   painter

2. How long was he a gardener?   3 years   3 months

3. Does he have any other experience?   yes   no

4. Can he take care of trees?   yes   no

5. Does he give his phone number?   yes   no

A. Study the Examples

I	can	fix car engines.
She	can't	
He		
We		
You		
They		

Can	she	fix car engines?
	you	

Yes,	she	can.
	you	
No,		can't.

COMPLETE THE DIALOG

Keon is talking to a career counselor about her skills and experience.
Write *can* or *can't*.

A I have a Class C license, so I _____*can*_____ drive a truck.

B _____ you drive a bulldozer or other construction equipment?

A No, I _____. But I can repair cars and trucks.

B Great. I think I _____ arrange some interviews for you.

PARTNER WORK

Talk with your partner about your job skills. Say all of the things you can do.
Talk about some things you can't do.

B. Study the Examples

I	was	a sales clerk.
She		
He		
We	were	sales clerks.
You		
They		

Was	he	a sales clerk?
Were	they	sales clerks?

Yes,	he	was.
No,		wasn't.

Yes,	they	were.
No,		weren't.

COMPLETE THE SENTENCES

Write *was* or *were*.

A What _____ was _____ your last job?

B I _____ a file clerk. What about you?

A I _____ a cook in my sister's restaurant.

B Really. _____ your sister also a cook?

A Yes, she _____ . We _____ both cooks.

She _____ the owner, too.

TEAM WORK

In a small group, talk about jobs you had in the past. Talk about some of your job responsibilities. Follow the example below.

I was a kitchen assistant. I can prepare meals and keep the kitchen clean. What about you?

C. Study the Examples

How long were you a home health aide?

From	1993	to	1997.
	May		August.

For	four years.
	three months.

COMPLETE THE DIALOG

Use the language in C.

A I was a mechanic in my country.

B Really? _____ How long _____ were you a mechanic?

A _____ 1987 to 1997.

B Oh, _____ ten years. That's a long time.

A Yes, I liked it. _____ were you a gardener?

B _____ five months. _____ March to August last year.

PARTNER WORK

Talk with your partner about your last job. Use the dialog above.

Unit 10

117

Reading and Writing

READ THE WANT ADS

Match each person with a job they can do. Write the letter of the ad.

HELP WANTED

(a) Experienced mechanics needed. Mike & Son's garage needs two mechanics. 2 years experience necessary. Call 555-3434 for an appointment.

(b) Do you like to get up early? The Gladtown Herald newspaper is looking for early morning delivery people. Must have a valid driver's license and a good driving record. No experience necessary. Apply in person at 12 Oceanview Drive.

(c) Global Airlines Are you interested in a good career? Global Airlines is looking for baggage handlers. We will train. Bilingual applicants preferred. Call 555-9090 for further information.

(d) Barbara's Bakery Experienced cake decorator needed. Must have references and 2 years' experience. Apply in person. 34 Riverside Drive.

(e) School Bus Drivers Wanted The City of Newton is looking for school bus drivers to begin in September. Class D license and good driving record required. There is a two-week training course before the job begins. Apply at Newton City Hall, 2100 Main Street.

(f) Animal Caretaker Do you like animals? The Citywide Animal Shelter is looking for animal caretakers to feed, water, exercise, and bathe animals. No formal experience required. Call 555-7394.

1. Reuben: loves animals; takes care of neighborhood pets when owners are away.

   Want ad: _____f_____

2. Hal: fixed cars at Mel's Garage from 1995 to 1997.

   Want ad: _____

3. Maria: has a class D driver's license.

   Want ad: _____

4. Elsa: speaks Spanish; likes physical activity.

   Want ad: _____

DISCUSSION

Can you do any of these jobs? Which ones are interesting to you? What skills do you need?

Unit 10

APPLICATION FOR EMPLOYMENT

PERSONAL INFORMATION

Name _____

Address _____

_____

Telephone _____ Social Security Number _____

What job are you applying for? _____

WORK EXPERIENCE

Job _____ Company _____

Address _____

Telephone _____ How long were you at this job? _____

• •

Job _____ Company _____

Address _____

Telephone _____ How long were you at this job? _____

READ AND SIGN

The above information is true and correct.

Signature _____ Date _____

PARTNER WORK

Practice answering these common interview questions.

1. Do you work well with others?

2. Are you organized?

3. What is your best job experience?

4. Talk about something you did that was difficult.

5. Describe your perfect job.

Now write down your answers. Use them to prepare for interviews.

Extension

COMPLETE THE SKILLS INVENTORY

Read the skills inventory. Check all the skills that you have.

WORK SKILLS

CHECK ALL THE SKILLS YOU HAVE.

Automotive
- ❏ change oil/tires
- ❏ make simple repairs
- ❏ do tune-ups
- ❏ fix flat tires
- ❏ pump gas

Clerical
- ❏ file
- ❏ keep records
- ❏ make copies
- ❏ type
- ❏ use a computer
- ❏ use a fax machine

Domestic
- ❏ cook/serve meals
- ❏ follow directions
- ❏ do housework

- ❏ shop for groceries
- ❏ wash/sort /iron clothes

Food Services
- ❏ clean tables
- ❏ cook
- ❏ serve meals
- ❏ take orders
- ❏ wash dishes

Gardening
- ❏ mow lawns
- ❏ pot/transplant plants
- ❏ water plants

Mechanical
- ❏ pack/wrap boxes
- ❏ put things together
- ❏ run machines
- ❏ work with tools

Retail
- ❏ use a cash register
- ❏ make change
- ❏ check inventory
- ❏ sell stock

Transportation
- ❏ drive a car/truck
- ❏ follow directions
- ❏ lift packages
- ❏ read maps

Other
- ❏ _____
- ❏ _____
- ❏ _____
- ❏ _____

ANSWER THE QUESTIONS

1. How many boxes did you check? _____

2. What job groups are they in? _____

3. How many different groups do you have skills in? _____

4. With these skills what jobs can you do? _____

_____

ON YOUR JOB   CultureNotes

There are many different ways to look for a job. You can look in the want ads or look for help-wanted signs at businesses. What are some other ways to find out about jobs? How did you find the job you have now? Talk to your classmates. How did they find their jobs?

Performance Check

Complete the activities. Go over your work with a partner or your teacher. Then complete the Performance Review on Page 122.

SKILL 1 DESCRIBE YOUR JOB SKILLS

Your partner or teacher is a job counselor. Tell him or her your job skills.

SKILL 2 READ A HELP-WANTED AD

Look at the want ad. Answer the questions.

> **Carpet Installer Needed**
> Must have experience. Apply in person at Superior Floor Coverings. 34 Tyler Street. Monday to Friday, 9 to 6.

1. What job is the ad for? _____

2. Do you need experience? _____

3. Do you apply in writing? _____

4. Would you like a job like this one? Why or why not? _____

_____

SKILL 3 FIGURE OUT THE BEST JOB FOR YOU

Look at the lists. Add to them if you wish. Choose the job that is best for you. Explain your choice to your partner or your teacher.

Skills	Jobs
Drive a truck	carpenter
Work well with tools	tailor
Like to work alone	auto mechanic
Like to work with people	delivery person
Know how to use a cash register	hairdresser
Can change oil in a car	painter

Complete the job application. Apply for a job you want.

APPLICATION FOR EMPLOYMENT

XYZ Company

PERSONAL INFORMATION

Name _____

Address _____

_____

Telephone _____ Social Security Number _____

What job are you applying for? _____

WORK EXPERIENCE

Job _____ Name of Company _____

Telephone _____ Supervisor's name _____

Dates of Employment: From _____ to _____

Performance Review

I can...

☐ **1.** describe my job skills.

☐ **2.** read help-wanted ads.

☐ **3.** figure out the best job for me.

☐ **4.** complete a job application.

DISCUSSION

Work with a team. How will these skills help you? Make a list.
Share your list with the class.

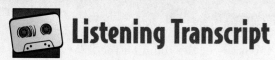

Listening Transcript

Listening (page 7)

LISTEN AND CIRCLE

Complete the conversations. Circle the letter.

1.
A: Hi, my name's Yolanda. I just started working here yesterday morning. I transferred from Manufacturing.
B: It's nice to meet you, Yolanda. I'm Clark.
C: What does Yolanda say next?

2.
A: Susan, do you know what time it is? I can't find my watch.
B: Sure. It's 3:30. Time to get ready for the dinner crowd.
B: Excuse me. I need to answer the phone.
C: How does Susan answer the phone?

3.
A: Good morning, Mr. Haines.
B: Good morning, Juliette. I'd like you to meet your new partner, Pablo. He'll be working with you to process the orders that have been coming in over the last few weeks.
C: What does Juliette say?

LISTEN AND CIRCLE

Listen to the conversations. Circle the correct information for each person.

1.
A: Hi, my name's Linda Marcos. I'm the new mail clerk.
B: Hi, I'm Eric Montoya. I work across town in the warehouse. It's nice to meet you.
A: Nice to meet you, too, Eric.

2.
A: Martin, I'd like you to meet Dale, our new plumber's helper.
B: Hi, Dale. Welcome to the job.
C: Thanks, Martin. I'm glad to be here.

A: Martin is the foreman on this job. He can help you get started.
C: Sounds great. I'm ready whenever you are.

3.
A: My name is Chen Wong. I'm here to meet with a job counselor.
B: Hi, Chen. I'm Marla Smith. I'm a job counselor. What can I do to help you?
A: I'm looking for a job where I can use my skills.
B: Good. Tell me a little about yourself.
A: Well, I'm from China. I speak Chinese and English, and I'm an experienced locksmith.
B: OK. Can you tell me about your education?

4.
A: Maria, this is Elena Rios, a new employee. She's from Mexico. She speaks Spanish.
B: It's nice to meet you. My name's Maria Santos. I'm from Honduras. I speak Spanish, too.
C: I'm happy to meet you. This looks like a great place to work.
B: Oh, it is. I really like working at the clinic.

Listening (page 19)

LISTEN AND CIRCLE

Circle the places you hear.

1.
A: Morning. I'm from Morrow Electric. I'm here to fix the lights in the kitchen. Can you tell me how to get there from here?
B: To the kitchen? Sure. Just walk down the hall. The kitchen is at the end of the hall on the right.
A: The end of the hall on the right. OK. Thanks.
B: No problem.

2.

A: Hey, Lew, I'm supposed to bring this coffee to Meeting Room 1. I've never been there before. Where is it?
B: Meeting Room 1?
A: Uh huh.
B: It's on the left, first door on the left.
A: First door on the left. Thanks, Lew.

3.

A: Excuse me. I think I'm lost. I'm looking for the parking lot. Can you help me?
B: The parking lot? It's right outside this door. Just go out this exit and you're there.
A: Oh, good. Now I just hope I can find my car.
B: Well, I can't help you there, but good luck.
A: Thanks. I think I'll need it.

4.

A: Excuse me. Can you tell me where the ladies' room is?
B: The ladies' room is down the hall. Turn left before Meeting Room 4. It's on the left.
A: I'm sorry. Could you repeat that?
B: Of course. Go down the hall. Then turn left before you get to Meeting Room 4. The ladies' room is on the left.
A: Thanks.
B: You're welcome.

5.

A: Phyllis, do you know where our orientation training is?
B: I know it's in Meeting Room 3. The problem is I don't know where Meeting Room 3 is.
A: Let me check the map. Hmm . . . it's down the hall on the right. It's the second door.
B: Are you sure?
A: Yes, look at the map. We walk down the hall. Meeting Room 3 is on the right. It's the second door on the right.
B: Now I see. Uh oh! Look at the time. We'd better hurry so we won't be late.

Write the name of the room on the floor plan. *(Play the tape or read the transcript of Listen and Circle aloud again.)*

Performance Check (page 25)

SKILL 2   **UNDERSTAND DIRECTIONS**

Listen and write the name of the room on the floor plan.

1.

A: Excuse me. I'm here to refill the vending machines and I need to get to the break room. Can you tell me how to get there?
B: To the break room? Sure. It's down the hall on the right. It's next to the meeting room. Don't worry. You can't miss it.
A: Down the hall on the right next to the meeting room? You're right. That sounds easy enough. Thanks.

2.

A: Hi, we're from The Paper Store and we've got a couple of cases of copier paper to deliver. We're supposed to take them to the supply room. Do you know where that is?
B: No problem. To get to the supply room, all you have to do is go down the hall and turn left. The supply room is the first door on the left.
A: Did you say it's on the left?
B: Uh huh. Go down the hall. Turn left and you'll see the supply room on the left.
A: Thanks.

U N I T ◆3

Listening (page 31)

LISTEN AND NUMBER

Listen to the instructions. Number the machine's parts in the order you use them.

A: Sara, can you help me fax this letter? This machine is a little different from the one I used in Production.
B: Sure. I'd be happy to. First, turn the machine on. Press the ON button.

A: OK, that makes sense. I press ON. Then what?
B: Put your letter into the document feeder.
A: Put it into the feeder like this?
B: That's right. Then, dial the fax number on the keypad.
A: Press these numbers to dial?
B: Yes, and you can check to be sure you pressed the right numbers by looking at the screen.
A: Look at the screen. That's a good idea.
B: Then, all you have to do is press SEND.
A: Press SEND and there it goes! Thanks.

LISTEN AND NUMBER

Number the steps in the correct order.

Before we begin, I'd like to thank everyone for coming in early today to learn how to use the new cash registers. The new registers were delivered and installed yesterday, so before we can open the store this morning, we need to do a little training. The new registers are not that different from the old ones. The first thing you do is put in your key. Turn the key to the ON position, like this. ON. Second, type in your employee number—mine is 4523—and press ENTER. ENTER is right here. After you press ENTER, the drawer will open. The last thing you do is close the drawer. Just push it closed. Now, as with our old cash registers...

Performance Check (page 37)

SKILL 1 FOLLOW INSTRUCTIONS

Listen to the instructions for putting paper in the copier. Number the steps in the correct order.

A: Can you help me with the copier?
B: Of course, Peter. What's the problem?
A: I need to add paper, but I don't know how.
B: It's easy. First open the paper drawer.
A: Which drawer? There are two.
B: Open the top drawer.
A: OK. I have it open. Now what?
B: Put some paper into the drawer.
A: About how much paper in the drawer?
B: About this much. Then push the paper under the tabs.
A: Push it down like this?

B: That's right. Now close the drawer. Make sure it's closed all the way.
A: Is that it?
B: Yes, that's right. Now press the red button. After you press the red button, it will take about thirty seconds for the copier to warm up.
A: Thanks.

UNIT 4

Listening (page 43)

LISTEN AND CIRCLE

Listen and circle the times you hear.

1.
A: Lin, can you work until 7:30 tonight? I know it's short notice, but Harold just called in sick.
B: 7:30? No problem.
B: Thanks.

2.
A: Are you working tonight?
B: Yes, but I don't start until 11:00. I'm working the late shift.
A: That's when I'm working too. See you at 11:00.

3.
A: Tina, I'd like to take a late lunch on Friday. Around 12:45.
B: 12:45's a little late, but I think we can work around you.
A: Thanks. I appreciate it.

4.
A: Buddy wants you to turn on the lights when you leave today.
B: That will be around 4:45. Is that OK?
A: I think 4:45's OK, but I'll check with Buddy.

5.
A: Do you know when they are coming to pick up these packages?
B: I'm not sure. Let me look at the schedule. They should be here about 10:15.
A: 10:50?
B: No, 10:15.

Listen and write Nora's work schedule on the calendar.

A: Big Mart. This is Sam. How can I help you?

B: Hi, Sam, it's Nora. I called to find out about my schedule for next week.

A: Let me check. I have you working on Monday from 12:00 to 6:00 and on Tuesday from 6:00 to 10:00.

B: Monday from 12:00 to 6:00 and Tuesday from 6:00 to 10:00. Anything else?

A: Can you come in on Friday?

B: Well, I have a doctor's appointment on Friday at 4:00. But I can come in around 5:30. I could work until 11:30.

A: That'll be fine. I'll put you down for Friday from 5:30 to 11:30. Thanks for calling.

B: See you Monday. Bye.

UNIT 5

Listening (page 55)

LISTEN AND WRITE

Listen to the orders. Write the number of items the customer says.

1.

A: Good morning, Order Department. How can I help you?

B: I'd like to order some tape.

A: Extra strength?

B: No, regular.

A: And how many rolls do you need?

B: About 12.

A: That's 12 rolls of regular tape. Your name?

B: Glen Sullivan. I'll be in this afternoon to pick them up.

2.

A: Alex, can you get this order from the warehouse? I need six monitors and three keyboards.

B: Sure. Did you say three keyboards?

A: Yes, three keyboards and six monitors.

3.

A: I'm off to pick up the paint order for the Haley project. It looks like we'll need five gallons of off-white paint and 15 gallons of dark green paint.

B: 15 gallons of dark green? Are you sure?

A: Let me check. Yes, that's right. 15 gallons of dark green and five gallons of off-white.

4.

A: First Call Couriers.

B: Yes, I have some packages that need to be delivered today.

A: How many packages are there?

B: Six small envelopes and two boxes.

A: I'm sorry. Can you repeat that, please?

B: Six envelopes and two boxes.

LISTEN AND WRITE

Listen to the customer place an order. Write the number of each item the customer wants.

A: Let me see if I have this correct, Ms. Bard. You want three boxes of light bulbs.

B: Yes, three boxes.

A: OK. That'll be $5.85 for the bulbs. Can I help you with anything else today?

B: Yes, I'd also like some extension cords and some switches.

A: How many would you like?

B: I'll need two switches and, umm . . . five . . . yes, five extension cords.

A: All right. The two switches come to $15.90, and the five extension cords are $12.50. Will that be all?

B: Oh, I almost forgot. I also need seven plugs.

A: And seven plugs. That'll be $27.65. Anything else, Ms. Bard?

B: No, that's all for now. What is my total?

A: Let's see. The light bulbs are $5.85, the two switches are $15.90, the extension cords are $12.50, and the plugs are $27.65. That comes to $61.90.

LISTEN AGAIN

Listen again and write the total cost for each item on the form. *(Play the tape or read the transcript of Listen and Write aloud again.)*

UNIT 6

Listening (page 67)

LISTEN AND CIRCLE

What are the rules about? Circle your answer.

1.

A: Good afternoon, Uma. Welcome to Green Technologies.

B: Thank you, Mr. Robinson.

A: I need to tell you about our rules for sick days. You're entitled to nine sick days a year.

B: Nine days. Who do I call when I'm sick?

A: Call your supervisor first thing in the morning.

2.

A: Brian, here's the time clock. Everyone at Rosetti Macaroni clocks in here. You punch in when you start work every morning and punch out when you leave every night.

B: What do I do if I forget to punch in or out?

A: Speak to your manager right away. Your manager's Ms. Valdosta. She can take care of it.

3.

A: What are you doing today, Elaine?

B: Shopping for some clothes. I just started work at the Garden Restaurant.

A: That's great.

B: Yeah. I need a white shirt and black pants. Then I'm off to the shoe store. I've got to get a pair of black shoes, too.

A: You might want to go to Allman's. I bought a really comfortable pair of black shoes there last week.

4.

A: King's Department Store has a rule about arriving late. It's very simple.

B: Really? What is it?

A: Well, you have to call if you're going to be late. And, if you arrive late three times, you get a warning.

B: Three times? I won't be late that often. I don't want to get a warning.

LISTEN AGAIN

Which rule goes with each company? Write the letter. *(Play the tape or read the transcript of Listen and Circle aloud again.)*

LISTEN ONCE MORE

Answer the questions. *(Play the tape or read the transcript of Listen and Circle aloud again.)*

UNIT 7

Listening (page 79)

LISTEN AND CIRCLE

Listen and circle the money amount you hear.

1.

A: Dora, can you look in the office supply catalog to see how much a new stapler is? Mine just broke.

B: Let me see . . . Oh, here's one like yours for $12.25. I can go out at lunch and pick one up for you if you'd like.

A: That would be great. Thanks.

B: Do you want to give me $12.25 in cash out of the register to pay for it?

A: Good idea. I'll get it for you.

2.

A: Lara just told me we have to mark down all the leather gloves. There's a sale starting tomorrow.

B: What are we marking them down to?

A: $8.99 a pair.

B: Only $8.99? I think I'll buy some for myself. Let me get my purse so I can write out a check.

3.

A: I need to talk to Gary about my paycheck.

B: Is there a problem?

A: Yes, there is. My check is for only $122.65. It looks like they forgot to include my vacation pay.

B: Let me see that . . . I don't think $122.65 is right, either. Why don't we take your check to Gary together and get this straightened out?

4.

A: Mario, we're out of small washers. Can you go to the plumbing supply store and get us some?

B: Sure, Joe.

A: Just take the money from petty cash. You shouldn't need much. The washers only cost about five cents each.

B: I'll be back in about half an hour. That was small washers, right?

A: Yes, the five-cent size.

LISTEN AGAIN

Write *cash* or *check. (Play the tape or read the transcript of Listen and Circle aloud again.)*

LISTEN AND WRITE

Listen and fill in the check.

A: That comes to $329.47. How would you like to pay?

B: By check. Do you take company checks?

A: We sure do.

B: Oh, good. Now how much did you say the total was?

A: $329.47.

B: Thanks. And I make the check out to...?

A: Johnson Art Supply.

B: Johnson Art Supply. J-O-H-N-S-O-N A-R-T S-U-P-P-L-Y.

A: Uh-huh.

B: Today's August 17, isn't it?

A: That's right. It's the seventeenth.

B: OK, August 17, 1999. Here's the check. Oops! I almost forgot to sign it. . . There you go.

UNIT 8

Listening (page 91)

LISTEN AND NUMBER

Listen to the instructions. Number the instructions in order.

How do you do? My name is Alex Brace and I work with the city fire department. I'm here at March Manufacturing today to go over the procedures to follow during a fire or fire drill. In case of a fire or fire drill, you will hear an alarm. When you hear the alarm follow these instructions:
1. Walk, do not run, to the nearest exit.
2. If you are the last person to leave a room or office, turn off the lights.
3. Be sure to close the door behind you.
4. Go down the nearest stairs. Do not use the elevators.

And finally, walk out of the building and to the northwest corner of the parking lot.

LISTEN AND CIRCLE

Listen to the emergencies. Who should you call? Circle the symbol.

1.

A: Are you all right? What happened?

B: I'm fine, but there was an accident on the factory floor. Lorna cut her hand.

2.

A: Hey, I smell smoke!

B: You're right. There's smoke coming from the boiler room.

3.

A: Doug, what's the matter?

B: I was putting more dye in the drum and some splashed onto my face.

A: That stuff's dangerous. It might be poison.

LISTEN AND WRITE

Listen to the emergency calls. What do you need to do?

1.

A: 911? My name is Lisa. I work at the Park City Library. A little boy just fell off a chair. He was trying to get a book.

B: Is he hurt?

A: I think he hurt his head.

B: Cover him with a blanket. Don't let him move. Wait for an ambulance. The paramedics will be there in a few minutes.

2.

A: Fire Department.

B: I'm at the Furniture Factory on Route 3. We smell smoke in the back of the building.

A: Tell everyone to leave the building now! Stay outside the building. We'll send a fire truck right away.

3.

A: 911 operator. What's your name, please?

B: Manuel Vargas. I work at a machine shop on Laurel Street.

A: What's the emergency?

B: My partner splashed some cleaning chemicals on his skin.

A: Find the container the chemicals came in. Call the poison control center right away. Their number is 555-1212.

4.

A: Express Couriers.

B: Mr. Stephanos, this is Diego. I was returning from my last delivery when my van broke down just outside of town.

A: Is anyone with you?

B: No, I'm by myself.

A: All right. Call a tow truck. Stay in the van until the tow truck or the police get there. Then call me back and tell me what's happening.

Performance Check (page 98)

SKILL 5 FOLLOW SAFETY INSTRUCTIONS

Listen to the instructions. Answer the questions. Circle *yes* or *no*.

Thank you all for coming to this month's workplace safety meeting. Today's topic is what to do in case of bad weather. First on the list is tornadoes. As you know, tornadoes are very dangerous storms. If there's a tornado in the area, you will hear a very loud, sharp warning signal. If you hear this signal, don't panic. Turn off any machines you're using and walk to the nearest elevator or stairs. Go down to the basement. Do not go out of the building. You will be much safer if you stay inside. Someone will be there to tell you where to wait until the all-clear signal. The all-clear signal will tell you when it's safe to go back to work.

UNIT 9

Listening (page 103)

LISTEN AND WRITE

Listen to the dialogs. Who can do the job? Write the letter of the picture.

1.

A: We've just signed three new customers. That means starting next week, we've got three more deliveries to make every day.

B: I guess we'd better start looking for another driver.

A: I think you're right. Do you know if anyone else in the company can drive a van?

B: I don't know, but we can always advertise in the paper for a driver if we have to.

2.

A: Suni, can you put this job posting up on the bulletin board in the employee lounge?

B: Sure. What kind of job is it?

A: It's a job in the warehouse. We're looking for someone who can do some heavy lifting and knows how to work carefully and safely.

B: I'm sure you'll be able to find someone who can do that.

3.

A: Jonathan, do you know any good mechanics?

B: Why? Do you have an opening at the garage?

A: Yes, I do. Tanya just got promoted to the front office. I need someone to take her place—someone who can fix cars and who works well with people.

B: My cousin knows a lot about cars. Let me talk to him and see if he's interested.

LISTEN AND CIRCLE

Circle the letter of the statement that describes each employee's performance.

1.

A: Cindy, I've called you in to talk about your work.

B: Is everything all right?

A: Generally you're doing a good job. You get to the restaurant on time every day, and that's very important to us.

B: Is there something I should be working on?

A: Well, yes. You need to serve your customers their meals a little more quickly.

B: Thanks for telling me. I'll try to work faster.

2.

A: It's time for your three-month evaluation, Enrique. Tell me, are you enjoying the new job?

B: Yes, I am. I really like talking to the customers.

A: I've noticed that you're usually very polite to your customers on the phone. But there is a problem with your paperwork. You need to be more careful when you write out your orders. Some of your orders are hard to read. You need to write more clearly.

B: Sure. I can do that.

3.

A: Hans, I'm pleased to tell you that you have the best safety record of anyone in the company.

B: Really?

A: Yes, you always drive safely and make all your deliveries on time. We think you're doing a super job.

B: Thanks, Ms. Ford. Is there anything I can do better?

A: Well, sometimes your uniform is a little messy. We expect all of our employees to dress neatly.

B: Oh, OK. I'll dress more neatly from now on.

4.

A: Hi, Maria. How are you doing this afternoon?

B: I'm fine, Mr. Lee.

A: Maria, I wanted to talk to you because I think we have a problem. I notice that you don't always enjoy working with other employees.

B: You're right. I prefer working alone when I can.

A: I understand, but it's important for you to work more closely with your team.

B: OK. Do you have any ideas?

A: Maybe you can team up with Arthur. He's easy to work with. I think it'll be good for you.

B: All right. I'd like to do that. Thanks.

U N I T 10

Listening (page 115)

LISTEN AND CIRCLE

Listen and circle the jobs the people are calling about.

1.

A: Consolidated Fan Company. How can I help you?

B: My name's Kevin Cho. I'm calling about the ad for a delivery truck driver.

A: Yes, that job is still available. We're looking for someone with at least two years experience.

B: I've been driving a delivery truck for Acme Products for the last three years.

A: That sounds good. Would you like to come in for an interview?

2.

A: Alvarez Salon. May I help you?

B: Yes, my name is Clara Hall. I saw a sign at school that says you're looking for a hairdresser.

A: Tell me, Clara, do you have your hairdresser's license yet?

B: No, not yet. I'm going to take the exam next week.

A: I'm sorry. We can't hire anyone without a license. But call us again when you pass the test.

3.

A: Green Landscaping. Human Resources.

B: Hello, my name's Carlos Ramos. I'm calling about your ad for an experienced gardener.

A: Hello, Mr. Ramos. Have you worked as a gardener before?

B: Yes, I have. I worked for Lakeside Landscaping for five years.

A: So you know how to use a lawn mower?

B: Yes, I have experience using many kinds of lawn mowers.

A: Excellent. Would you like to come in for an interview?

4.

A: Job Hotline. This is Berta. How can I help you?

B: My name's Suzy. I just received my nurse's aide certificate from the community college, and I'm looking for a job. Are there any jobs available?

A: Yes, there are. I have several openings for nurse's aides. Would you like to come in to talk about the jobs?

LISTEN AGAIN

Read the questions about their training and skills. Circle the answers. *(Play the tape or read the transcript of Listen and Circle aloud again.)*

LISTEN AND CIRCLE

Pablo Bueno is calling about a job. Read the questions. Circle the answers.

A: Lawn and Garden Company. May I help you?

B: Yes, I'm calling about the gardener's job in the newspaper. My name is Pablo Bueno.

A: Hi. My name is Lilia Silverman. I'm going to ask you some questions, get a little information, and then have someone call you back. Is that OK?

B: Sure.

A: First, can you spell your name for me?

B: It's Pablo, P-A-B-L-O, Bueno, B-U-E-N-O.

A: Tell me a little about yourself, Mr. Bueno.

B: Well, I was a gardener for a company that manages large apartment buildings and houses.

A: Oh, for how long?

B: Three months. It was a summer job. And I have some experience working in my own garden, too.

A: That's good. Can you take care of trees?

B: I don't have any experience taking care of trees, but I'm sure I can learn.

A: Well, that's about it for now. The only other thing I need is your phone number.

B: It's 555-2133.

A: 555-2133. Thanks. Someone will call you back soon.

B: Thank you.

Listening Transcript

Vocabulary

UNIT 1

name
address
city
state
zip code
telephone number
Social Security number

hi
good-bye
good morning
good afternoon
good evening

country
language
employee

UNIT 2

break room
entrance
exit
hall
ladies' room
office
meeting room
men's room
parking lot
rest rooms
supply room

left
right
across from
between
next to

go
turn
walk

UNIT 3

cash register
coffee maker
computer
copier
document feeder
fax machine
keypad
printer
screen
vacuum cleaner

start button
stop button

close
copy
open
plug in
press
push
send
turn off
turn on

UNIT 4

part time
full time
overtime
shift
hours
holiday
day off

late
early

day
date
month
year

appointment
calendar
schedule

UNIT 5

apology
complaint
customer
order
problem
service

discount
exchange
guarantee
refund

no problem
of course
sure

UNIT 6

break
sick day
rules

flexible
pleasant
polite
punctual

late
on time

certainly
of course

clock in
clock out
punch in
punch out

Miss
Mr.
Mrs.
Ms.

excuse me
pardon me
please
thank you
thanks

UNIT 7

account
cash
check
paycheck
tax
time card
W-4 form

penny
nickel
dime
quarter
dollar

charge
deposit
endorse
sign

UNIT 8

accident
emergency
fire
fire alarm
poison control center
tornado
911

fever
flu
headache
injury
stomachache
toothache

ankle
arm
chest
ear
eye
finger
foot
hand
head
knee

leg
mouth
neck
nose
shoulder
stomach
throat
toe
wrist

burn
cut
hurt

UNIT 9

duty
feedback
responsibility
skill
task
training manual

evaluate
teach

negative
positive

UNIT 10

experience
job application
license
skills inventory
training
want ad

assistant
baggage handler
baker
bus driver
carpenter
cook
child care worker
construction worker

delivery driver
file clerk
gardener
grocery clerk
hairdresser
mechanic
medical technician
nurse's aide
painter
plumber
police officer
sales clerk
secretary
tailor
truck driver

apply
drive
fix
paint
prepare
repair

Vocabulary